Anonymous

The City of Saint Paul

Anonymous

The City of Saint Paul

ISBN/EAN: 9783337341084

Printed in Europe, USA, Canada, Australia, Japan

Cover: Foto ©ninafisch / pixelio.de

More available books at **www.hansebooks.com**

AND THE

Commercial, Railway and Financial

Metropolis of the Northwest.

ISSUED BY

THE ST. PAUL CHAMBER OF COMMERCE,

INCLUDING THE ANNUAL REPORT OF THAT BODY FOR
THE YEAR ENDED DECEMBER 31, 1883.

[OFFICIAL.]

SAINT PAUL:
THE PIONEER PRESS PUBLISHING COMPANY
1884.

State Capitol

Summary of Salient Features.

St. Paul, Minnesota, March 15, 1884.

The following tabulated synopsis of the principal facts and figures given in this pamphlet will prove useful for general reference, and may enable the reader to judge quickly of the many reasons why it will prove profitable to examine closely the opportunities now presented by St. Paul (detailed within these pages) to all persons who desire to take advantage of the present phenomenal growth of the city and the wonderful development of the Northwest:

POPULATION OF ST. PAUL.

Number of inhabitants in 1850.. 840
Number of inhabitants in 1860.. 10,600
Number of inhabitants in 1870.. 20,300
Number of inhabitants in 1880.. 41,498
Number of inhabitants in 1883..100,000

Increase in population in past three years, 112 per cent.

ST. PAUL'S WHOLESALE BUSINESS.

YEAR.	No. of Establishments.	No. Employes.	Amount of Sales.
1870...			$9,813,000
1881...	223	3,180	46,535,999
1882...	276	4,684	66,628,494
1883...	325	5,815	72,048,771

Receipts of Customs—

	Amount.
1870..	$11,821.56
1883..	64,016.06

Commercial Agency Figures—

Dun & Co. place capital of 289 firms at..$54,970,000
Bradstreet's agency reports that there has been no failure among St. Paul Wholesale houses in three years.

RETAIL AND GENERAL BUSINESS.

Number of new concerns established in 1883..608
Capital of 1,669 houses reported by Dun & Co. averaging over $5,000 each (including wholesale)..$73,490,000
Ratio of increase of population for past year exceeds ratio of increase in number of new retail concerns 33 per cent, showing that retail business is not overdone.

ST. PAUL'S MANUFACTURES.

YEAR.	No. Establishments.	No. Employes.	Value of Products.
1870	88	985	$1,611,378
1878	332	3,117	6,150,000
1880	542	6,029	11,606,824
1881	667	8,188	15,466,201
1882	694	12,267	22,390,589
1883	758	13,979	25,885,471

THE BANKS OF ST. PAUL.

Capital and surplus of St. Paul banks, State and National $6,930,132.00
Capital of all other banks in Minnesota combined 6,085,350.00

Capital of St. Paul's National banks, Dec. 31, 1883 .... $4,700,000.00
Capital of all other National banks in Minnesota combined 4,451,000.00

Excess of capital of St. Paul National banks over all others in the State $349,000.00

Individual deposits in St. Paul National banks $9,473,146.22
Individual deposits in all other Minnesota National banks combined 7,563,203.78

Excess of St. Paul National bank deposits over those of all other National banks in
Minnesota combined $1,909,942.44

Capital of St. Paul National banks $4,700,000.00
Capital of all National banks in State of Wisconsin 4,035,000.00

Excess of capital of St. Paul National banks over all National banks in Wisconsin $735,000.00

COMPARISON OF RESOURCES OF ST. PAUL NATIONAL BANKS WITH THOSE OF OTHER
CITIES, AS PER OCTOBER (1883) REPORT OF THE NATIONAL
COMPTROLLER OF THE CURRENCY:

Cities.	No. of Banks.	Resources.	Cities.	No. of Banks.	Resources.
1—New York	48	$457,217,563	10—St. Paul	5	$16,935,096
2—Boston	54	192,020,596	11—New Orleans	7	16,046,934
3—Philadelphia	32	117,776,564	12—Albany	7	15,073,754
4—Chicago	11	74,463,102	13—Louisville	9	14,517,043
5—Pittsburg	23	46,344,686	14—Detroit	5	13,561,914
6—Baltimore	17	45,962,456	15—Milwaukee	3	7,263,784
7—Cincinnati	13	38,102,538	16—Washington	5	4,975,391
8—Cleveland	7	18,111,481	17—San Francisco	1	4,101,582
9—St. Louis	6	17,308,914			

Capital of St. Paul banks, 1870 .... $900,000
Capital of St. Paul banks, 1882 3,250,000
Capital of St. Paul banks, 1883 5,550,000

Increase in capital of St. Paul banks in one year $2,300,000

Exchange sold in 1870 .... $16,637,563
Exchange sold in 1883 (by National banks alone) 163,683,070

ST. PAUL'S RAILWAYS.

Number of trunk lines now running trains into St. Paul 10
Number of new roads now building to or from St. Paul 5
Number of roads extending toward St. Paul soon to seek this city 5
Number of passenger trains in and out of St. Paul daily 164
Miles of road operated in the St. Paul system 13,611

Every hour of the day witnesses departure of through trains for Chicago, St. Louis, Omaha,
Winnipeg, Lake Superior points and the Pacific coast.
St. Paul is the principal terminus, general headquarters, site of shops, etc., of the following roads:
Northern Pacific, St. Paul, Minneapolis & Manitoba; St. Paul & Duluth; Chicago, St. Paul,
Minneapolis & Omaha.

Number of miles of railway added to the St. Paul system within three years 7,200
Number of miles of road added to St. Paul system in 1883........................... 1,319
Cost of said construction.. $25,836,500
Cost of railway improvements made within city limits of St. Paul in 1883................... 1,573,000

COUNTRY TRIBUTARY TO ST. PAUL.

Territory.	No. Square Miles.
North half of Wisconsin..	27,000
Minnesota...	81,259
Portion of Iowa..	15,000
Dakota..	150,932
Wyoming...	97,883
Montana..	145,776
Idaho..	86,300
Oregon..	95,274
Washington...	69,994
Manitoba...	151,411
Total area...	923,829

Total area of the United States...2,936,166

Area tributary to St. Paul is equal to more than one-fourth of the entire area of the United States, and comprises the best agricultural, grazing, timber and mineral lands of the entire continent. Is greater than combined area of Germany, France, Norway, Sweden, Holland and Denmark.

ST. PAUL'S BUILDING GROWTH.

Bradstreet's report for the building season of 1883 places St. Paul fourth in the list of American cities, New York, Chicago and Cincinnati alone leading, as follows:

New York	....$37,217,000
Chicago	12,780,000
Cincinnati	11,000,000
St. Paul (eight months only)	9,580,000
Minneapolis	8,310,000
Cleveland	3,750,000

UPBUILDING SINCE 1880:

YEAR.	No. Business Houses.	No. Residences.	Public Buildings.	Total.	Aggregate Cost.
1881....................	139	1,000	13	1,161	$4,571,700
1882....................	234	2,178	29	2,481	8,399,000
1883....................	434	3,124	49	3,607	11,938,950
Total in 3 years,	807	6,302	91	7,209	$24,909,650

Number of miles of business frontage erected within the past year...............................2

REAL ESTATE.

Sales during	No. Deeds.	Consideration.
1883...	4,874	$12,981,331
1882...	4,447	9,354,841
Increase of 1883 over 1882...............................	427	$3,626,490

HEALTH OF ST. PAUL.

St. Paul, death rate per 1,000 of population.. ....11.65
New York, death rate per 1,000 of population..24.36
Boston, death rate per 1,000 of population..20.43
Average for the world, death rate per 1,000 of population..........................22.00

EDUCATIONAL FACILITIES.

Number of public school buildings completed...17
Number of public school buildings to be built this year................................ 5
Cost of school buildings completed...$503,500
Amount to be expended in 1884.. 100,000
Number of private schools and academies...24
Colleges: Macalester College, Hamline University.
Public school fund of Minnesota...$6,000,000
Public school fund when lands are all sold... 15,000,000

Public school lands comprise two sections out of each township, or one-eighteenth of the total area of Minnesota.

Number volumes in St. Paul Public Library, State Library and State Historical Library...30,000

CHURCHES AND BENEVOLENT SOCIETIES.

Number of churches in St. Paul...70
Number of benevolent societies and institutions...23

MISCELLANEOUS STATISTICS.

Number of Steamboats running on St. Paul lines...17
Number of Building Societies in St. Paul........ 26
Capital of Building Societies in St. Paul $10,000,000
Number of houses built through building societies in 1883..............................400

Latest report of Postmaster General shows that the business of the St. Paul office is larger than that of any city of similar size in the United States.

Yearly income of postoffice has increased from $81,299.92 in 1879, to $190,907.36 in 1833.

Over thirty beautiful lakes lie within ten miles of the city limits of St. Paul, affording innumerable sites for romantic summer homes for residents of the city. Hourly trains run from St. Paul, in the season, to the favorite and fashionable summer resorts, White Bear Lake and Lake Minnetonka.

St. Paul possesses the largest and finest Opera House in the Northwest.

When Gen. Grant saw the procession in St. Paul in honor of the opening of the Northern Pacific railway he exlaimed: " I have seen many grand processions, civic and military, but such a display as this of a city's industries I have never seen."

"I think the growth of St. Paul in the next twenty-five years will far exceed that of the past twenty-five years."—HENRY VILLARD.

In January last, Rufus Hatch said: " I know the Northern Pacific to be a splendid road, and it is coming out all right if rightly managed. It's a magnificent thing for St. Paul, and will bring that city all the business of the Northwest. Since the excursion over the Northern Pacific and to the Yellowstone, I have cut out twelve long editorial and local notices of that region from the London Telegraph, that reaches 100,000 persons a day; ten from the London Times and nine from the London Post. They are still keeping it up. So are the German papers. It is worth millions to the Northwest. Foreign capitalists will bring $100,000,0 0 into the country to invest there this year. They know about the country now. I believe it is the place to put money, and bought a large block of land last month."

Builders of business blocks in St. Paul are receiving in rentals from 15 to 25 per cent on their investments.

Builders of medium residences are securing in rentals from 18 to 28 per cent on their investments.

Workingmen are sure of constant employment at good wages in St. Paul.

Capital can find better opportunities (and equally safe) for investment in St. Paul than in any other city in America.

The growth of St. Paul during the past three years, in all ways that combine to make a metropolis, has never been equaled by the development of any other city of the United States. The average increase in the aggregate of commercial, industrial, railway and financial interests, has exceeded 100 per cent since 1881.

Introductory.

The purpose of this pamphlet is to present reliable and concise information concerning the city of St. Paul and the various sections of country tributary to it. The publication is by the authority and under the auspices of the St. Paul Chamber of Commerce. It is intended that the reader shall derive, from the facts presented, information which will lead to specific results of importance to the individual. In any event the pamphlet will repay careful perusal.

What would it have been worth, thirty years ago, to the then average business man or capitalist if he could have forseen the growth of Chicago to its present proportions? How inestimable that glance into futurity would have been—the presentation of an unlimited opportunity for the acquirement of wealth and position! And it is the very purpose of these pages to indicate to the thoughtful mind just such an opportunity as was presented by the great Western metropolis a score or more of years ago. Herein the capitalist will discover a field for investment such as no city on the American continent now presents; and such as Chicago alone has presented in the past. Herein will be clearly defined to the manufacturer a comparatively unoccupied plant backed by a commercial development which has already made St. Paul the metropolis of the Northwest. Before the wholesaler and jobber in trade will be spread out the most rapidly-developing territory of the country, greater in area and richer in natural resources than any region tributary to any other American city. To the retailer will be given official figures to prove that St. Paul's population has increased over 100 per cent within the past three years, while the increase in retail establishments has been less than 35 per cent. The professional man will discover in almost every line of argument and in every figure presented, cogent reason why his vocation may be plied to advantage and advancement in St. Paul. The artisan of every trade, representing either skilled or unskilled labor, may perhaps profit (proportionately at least) as much as any other reader by a thorough study of these pages; for he will find herein the record of constant demand, at fair wages, for his labor, coupled with a health-giving climate, the best free school facilities, and opportunities for securing cheap and comfortable homes. The young man or woman, yet undecided as to a future home or business, will find the facts presented of special importance; life success to individuals of this class may be pointed out, where heretofore the effort to discover a proper place and sphere has failed. To the person of means who has retired from active business pursuits and desires most of all to locate permanently where health and pleasure may be best and most easily secured, this pamphlet will prove important and interesting. There is yet another class that may derive hope and benefit from these pages — the army of invalids that, like Ponce de Leon, search only for the fountain of health and are led hither and thither by false statements and theories, given as mere declarations by irresponsible localities or individuals. All classes will learn that St. Paul possesses exceptional educational advantages, not only in public schools but in the different universities and colleges here located; and all who read these pages carefully — not excepting citizens of St. Paul — will discover new facts, relative to the Northwest and its metropolis, that may be of immediate value and service.

All statements made herein, and figures given, are vouched for by the St. Paul Chamber of Commerce, through a select committee to which was assigned the duty of editing the material collated by the Secretary of the Chamber in preparing his annual report of the business interests of St. Paul for the year ended December 31, 1883.

Site of St. Paul.

The corporate limits of St. Paul embrace the head of navigation on the Mississippi, and comprise an area of twenty-one square miles located on both banks of the great river. Being the head of navigation on the Mississippi, St. Paul is, therefore, the head of navigation of by far the grandest and most extended river system in the world. It was this consideration which led William H. Seward to say, as long ago as 1860, while standing in the doorway of the state capitol in St. Paul:

"I find myself for the first time upon the high land in the center of the continent of North America, equi-distant from the waters of Hudson bay and the Gulf of Mexico. Here is the place— the central place—where the agricultural products of this region of North America must pour out their tributes to the world. I have cast about for the future and ultimate seat of power of North America. I looked to Quebec, to New Orleans, to Washington, San Francisco and St. Louis for the future seat of power. But I have corrected that view. I now believe that the ultimate, last seat of government on the great continent will be found somewhere not far from the spot on which I stand, at the head of navigation of the Mississippi river."

Mr. Seward's prediction, however, was based upon the fact of St. Paul's being the head of navigation of the river system of the country, and did not take into consideration the much more important fact—which was unknown or unappreciated at the time—that the city's location was a natural doorway to a region of greater extent and resources than any yet developed on the continent. The advantages of this position are just beginning to be thoroughly understood, and the result thus far is an increase of 112 per cent in population within three years, the rush of railways to secure entrance and terminal facilities here, the influx of wholesale houses, the upbuilding of manufactories, and a constant tide of all the concomitants that create a metropolis. Now that the advantages of St. Paul's location are beginning to be understood, the knowledge will grow with a constantly increasing ratio, that insures a more sudden metropolitan development than has ever occurred in this or any other country. Indeed, if a city of St. Paul's population in 1880 (41,000) can more than double in three years, what may not the next decade accomplish? It is difficult to fully comprehend the wonderful recent growth of the city, but the statistics presented in this pamphlet will afford some assistance in arriving at an understanding of the phenomenon.

St. Paul's location has already been fully recognized by the railway companies, and from this point radiates every line of road that is seeking northwestern business. Commerce and manufactures are learning a lesson from the railways and vie with them in securing advantageous locations in the new trade center. The supremacy of St. Paul's position, which was denied four years ago, is suddenly an acknowledged fact. There can be no other controling business center for the Northwest. This the moneyed power sees with its clear vision, and hence the capital of St. Paul banks exceeds the combined capital of all the other financial institutions of the State, including those of every other city and village. Trade and commerce note the broad expanse of river and the daily arrival of steamboats in their season, and argue that therein is eternal protection against possible adverse combination of railway traffic rates. Population marks the healthfulness of St. Paul's site, and is content with its guarantee of vigorous life and consequent prosperity.

St. Paul's site is made romantic and beautiful by circling hills that skirt level plateaus and form natural boundaries between the commercial and residence portions of the city. At this point the Mississippi's course is nearly due east until the eastern limits of the city are reached, when the river turns quickly on its southern way to the gulf. This course divides St. Paul into two portions which are connected by a costly and substantial iron bridge. The major part of the city is on the eastern bank of the river, and this portion is subdivided by two considerable streams flowing down from the north and creating valleys which are natural rights of way for railway lines through the hill barriers to their course east, northeast, north, northwest or west. The photographic views of St. Paul, to be found on the title page and on the back of the cover of this pamphlet, will give the reader a far better idea of the general site of the city than any pen picture could possibly do. The title page represents that portion of the city seen from a point of view where the railway lines from the east and north enter the Union depot grounds, and leaves out altogether the eastern district and the west side of the city ; while the view given on the back of the cover presents more of a bird's-eye effect, and was taken from the high hills in West St. Paul. The topography of the site of the city is such that rarely beautiful residence localities may ever be preserved close to the business heart of the town, while there is abundance of room for commercial growth in lines between the two principal residence districts.

It is difficult to conceive of a more beautiful and useful combination of plateaus and elevations, upon which to build a great city, than is here presented. The business portions are convenient to the river, while elevated against any possible danger from flood. Foundations, in a large part of the business district, may be hewed out of the solid rock. The principal residence localities afford magnificent views of the romantic valley of the Mississippi, and of the beautiful lake region north of the city. Pure water, perfect drainage and salubrious atmosphere combine with Nature's picturesque effects of landscape to make the site of St. Paul all that its people can desire.

St. Paul's Wholesale Trade.

The magnitude of St. Paul's wholesale and jobbing trade establishes beyond question the city's claim to the position of commercial metropolis of the Northwest. The largest and strongest dry goods, grocery, drug, paper and fur concerns in the Mississippi valley outside of Chicago are permanently established in St. Paul ; and in the lines specified only one or two of the great houses of Chicago overshadow those of this city. The general solidity and character of St. Paul's wholesale houses have for many years been the quiet boast of citizens, yet it is only within three or four years that the volume of business transacted has attracted the special attention of the commercial world. Since 1881, however, St. Paul has more and more occupied the Western and Northwestern field, until now Chicago and St. Louis no longer claim supremacy in this region, but are content to take what they can get in an even and well contested struggle. It is generally conceded, by those interested, that the ratio of business increase enjoyed by St. Paul commercial houses within the past three years, if continued for the next decade, will place this city beyond possible rivalry in the vast region naturally tributary to it. The growth of business can only be understood or appreciated by study of the official figures which have been collated every year since 1865, when there were five or six concerns that claimed to do a jobbing trade. In that year the largest amount sold by a single firm barely reached $100,000. In 1870 the total trade reached $9,813,000, and the figures were a standing subject of favorable comment and admiration. It was not until the close of 1881, however, that the figures presented a really large showing, resulting in a total of $46,555,999. Then began the wonderful development, which has never been surpassed by any American trade center, that swelled the figures of the wholesale trade of St. Paul to $72,048,771 in 1883. Such, in few words and general terms, is what St. Paul has thus far accomplished in a commercial way ; and it is but a hint of the possibilities of the future.

RESULTS THAT MAY BE ANTICIPATED.

St. Paul has, then, during the past year—despite the best energies of Chicago, Milwaukee and St. Louis—distributed $72,048,771 worth of goods throughout Northern Wisconsin, Minnesota, Dakota and the far West ; a vast domain on the very threshold of development ; a region of incalculable possibilities, but as yet more in its infancy than the territory which has made Chicago, was thirty years ago ; an empire of natural wealth of forest, field and mine greater than any city on this continent ever had to its own exclusive advantage. St. Paul is, by geographical location, the one absolute gateway to this field of future greatness in wealth and population. Northwestern trade and commerce cannot flow round St. Paul—the railways have settled that point forever—but must ever concentrate at this point. And it is not alone the trade and traffic of the territory east of the Rocky Mountains (which up to this time has been the sole dependence) which is to make this city one of the mighty commercial centers of the nation, but, situate midway between the ports of entry on the Pacific of the products of the eastern empires of the old world, and the ports of export on the Atlantic, St. Paul becomes by its very position the natural middleman between the East and the West. Whatever, then, the immense region embraced in Oregon, Washington Territory, Idaho, Wyoming, Montana, Dakota, Minnesota, Northern Wisconsin and the British provinces of Manitoba and the Northwest Territory, may in the future become (aggregating more than one-fourth the entire area of the United States), St. Paul will be its chief mart and metropolis.

There is another important factor in the question of St. Paul's future supremacy as a commercial center ; and that is its position at the head of navigation on the most extended river system of the world. If rail rates east and south should ever become an imposition, the products of the Northwest may easily and quickly secure market by river to New Orleans and the Gulf of Mexico ; Louisville, Cincinnati and Pittsburg, even, are accessible by water route. This single condition secures immunity forever, to the commercial interests of St. Paul, from any form of freight rate extortion. But St. Paul's position at the head of navigation on the Mississippi has a grander purpose to serve in the future than standing guard over groundless fears of extortion ; for, year by year as the great valley of the Mississippi prospers and becomes more and more populous, so will the improvement of nature's highway be pushed forward until it shall become the main route of commerce between the North and the South—and St. Paul will be the great Northern depot of all the river traffic.

Upon the subject of St. Paul's future position as the commercial metropolis of the Northwest, and the movement of the seat of trade supremacy from the East to the West, the St. Paul *Daily Pioneer Press* recently gave the following editorial utterance :

The present generation has seen the preponderance of population, of production, and of political power cross the Alleghanies. It is now witnessing a daily transference of the seat of manufactures from East to West, and corresponding changes in every department of business are sure to follow, where they have not already been wrought. One of the most important of these, though one which has up to this time been too lightly noticed or understood, is the gradual but steady and certain movement of the heart centers of the jobbing trade of the country to the West. As surely as the railroad has superseded the waterway as a means of quick communication; as surely as Ohio first, and then Minnesota, distanced New York in the amount of their wheat production ; as surely as Chicago sought and won from New York, Boston and Philadelphia control of the markets of the Mississippi valley, so surely is the same tide of progress sweeping onward, and bearing to St. Paul the full measure of that commercial supremacy which is hers by right of continental location, and which the inevitable laws that govern the competition of demand and supply are now working out.

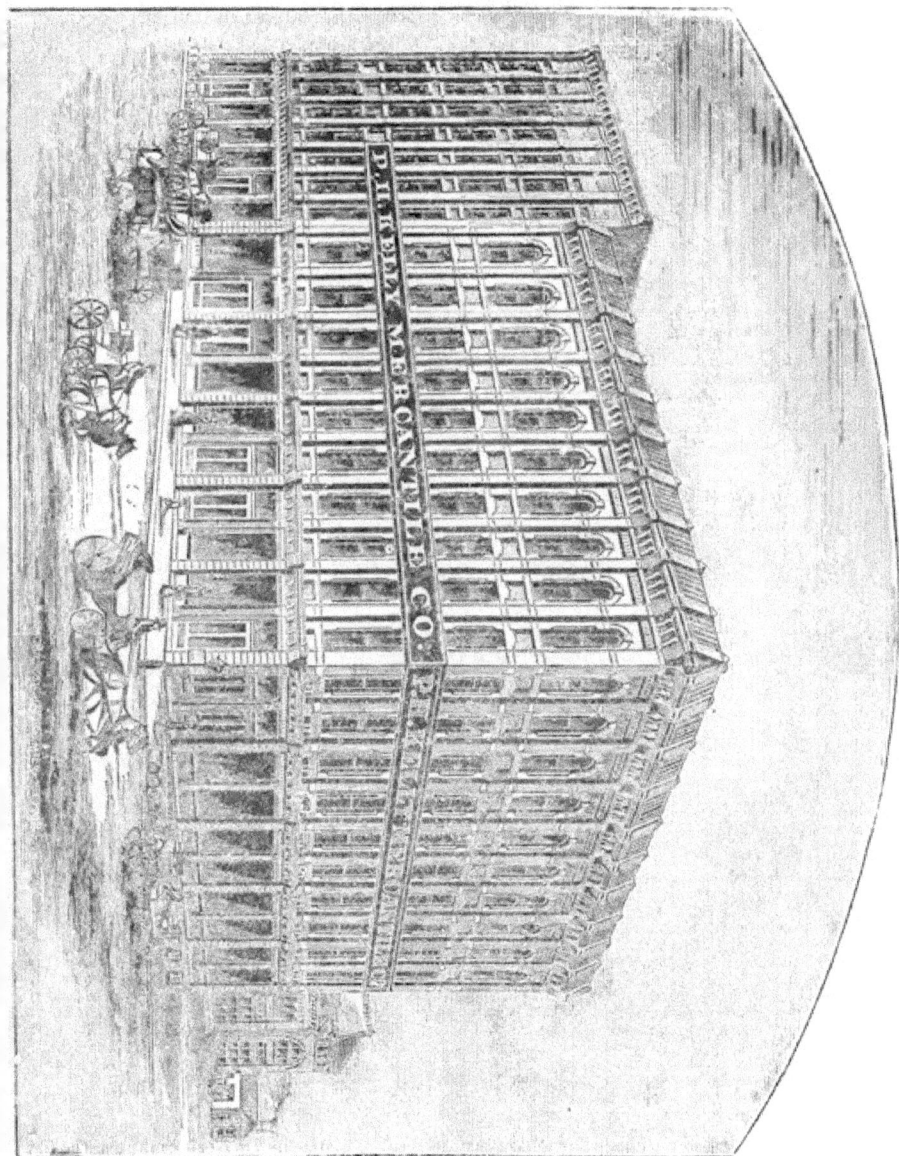

The above cut represents the great wholesale house of the P. H. Kelly Mercantile Co., one of the largest grocery houses in the United States. It is situated at the southeast corner of Third and Wacouta streets.

It will not be difficult to show what we mean by this assertion, to illustrate the action of the forces that rule the empire of the trade, fixing its capital and its boundaries, and to demonstrate that to-day St. Paul is by every consideration the leading center for the jobbing trade of the entire Northwest, the market where it will prove to be the pecuniary advantage of every dealer in this territory to purchase his supplies. A distinct confession of the truth of this proposition, as well as an intimation of the causes that underlie it, from an authority most reluctant to acknowledge it, and most actively hostile to the establishment here of a great jobbing business, will be found in the following editorial admission of the Chicago *Tribune*: "Chicago is changing. It is perfectly obvious that something like the same shift is taking place in our trade that carried the jobbing trade of the West from New York to Chicago. The interior jobber west of us is taking to himself the local business of his locality, and the jobbing business that used to be done here is merging into the wholesale supply of the western jobber."

Taking the above at its clear and inevitable meaning, it is translatable into the simple and truthful statement that what Chicago became to New York, and the other commercial centers of the Eastern seaboard, St. Paul is now becoming to both Chicago and the Atlantic cities. To the former belongs the business of supplying the needs of the great Northwest. To the latter belongs the business which is legitimately theirs, as coming from a surrounding and directly tributary territory, together with the supplying of the jobbers who have taken business into their own hands at the new center. The change must be accepted with as good a grace as possible, since it cannot be escaped. It is not many years since the Eastern cities made a desperate stand against the transfer of the jobbing business of the West, formerly a profitable and fabulously promising branch of their trade, to Chicago merchants. The fight was short, sharp, and decisive, and the Western city was victorious, as the destiny of geographical position and the play of natural forces had willed that it should be. The cities which saw the new trade wrested from their grasp were forced to confine themselves more strictly to the demands of the ever more densely peopled New England, Middle and Southern States, while they remained the great supply depot for imported and locally manufactured goods, from whose stores the Western wholesaler might draw at need. Precisely the same change is falling upon Chicago, with the acknowledged removal of the jobbing center still farther to the West. St. Paul is taking its place in the succession; and its wholesale business, its opportunities to those engaged in that business, and the superior advantages which it can offer over all competing points to-day to the buyer, designate it as both now and to be the entrepot and sovereign of the New Northwest.

It will be interesting to look a little into the causes which are working this transformation, that we may both see and understand its origin and its proof. Let us suppose a simple case of competition between St. Paul and Chicago for the trade of a merchant of the Northwest, and it will at once appear that the advantage that turns the scale is on the side of the Minnesota distributing point. Assume for the moment what we will presently show to be far from the fact, that the Eastern manufacturer sells his goods, delivered at his factory, at a fixed price to all customers. Then the Chicago jobber pays freight on his purchases to Chicago, and the St. Paul jobber must pay on his, additional charges from Chicago to St. Paul. Where, now, shall the retail merchant of the Northwest lay in his stock? If he buys in Chicago he, too, must pay freight charges from Chicago westward, and these charges will be such as are imposed upon a mixed consignment, which must be shipped under the conditions prevailing in the season of purchase. If he buys in St. Paul, the common impression is that the freight from Chicago will be added to the price and charged in the bill, thus making the totals equal. But this prevailing idea is a false one. There are three circumstances which prevent this equalization of totals, which put the St. Paul jobber at an advantage as compared with all others, and enable him to wrest from Chicago the business belonging to the territory adjacent to or west of him, precisely as Chicago wrested its business from New York. In the first place, the freight charges to which he is subject are less than those necessarily imposed upon a small purchaser shipping from Chicago. Carrying a heavy stock and buying for the trade, all seasons are his own. Heavy freight can be brought hither by the lakes at a substantial decrease o. cost. Iron from Pittsburg may be sent down the Ohio and brought up the Mississippi with the same result. All the advantages that belong to a large shipper over a small one, that inhere in a business able to take advantage of the choice of times and routes of transit, to offset rail with water transportation and make a brief cutting of rates by rivals do service for the future are at his command. For this reason it is a true and general principle that the difference between the first cost of an article bought of a wholesaler in St. Paul and in Chicago is always less than the cost to the buyer of shipping it from one point to the other. Therefore the constant advantage is on the side of St. Paul, and the bulk of trade inevitably shifts in answer to the operation of this ever-acting force. In the second place, our merchants can afford to make lower terms, and content themselves with smaller margins of profit on the few lines of goods to which the foregoing argument may not apply, both because these are so decidedly a minority, and because there are other lines where the Western distributing point has so tremendous an advantage over the Eastern that resistance is practically useless. And this brings us to the third consideration, one not so generally known outside of business circles, which i steadily driving the jobbing trade to the Western center in spite of all that cities farther east an do to retain it.

This final and controlling fact is the competition of manufacturers, by which the burden of freight charges is lifted from the consumer, from the retailer and from the jobber, and assumed by the maker of the article himself. For years there has been growing up a practice by which the manufacturers of certain lines of goods agree to deliver their wares at a fixed price to purchasers, not at the factory, but at any one of a number of important distributing points throughout the country. This, it will be seen at a glance, eliminates the element of freight charges from jobbing competition, or rather adds it to the overwhelming disadvantages with which the Eastern jobber must contend. For it is evident that, if a certain commodity is furnished to the wholesale merchants of St. Paul at exactly the same price as to those of Chicago, the latter are out of the race.

Were they even to determine desperately to pay the whole cost of freight from their warehouses to the retail store, they could not keep the trade, because any terms that they may choose to make can be met, and still the balance of freight between the two cities is against them. It is this fact that makes Chicago so freely acknowledge and accept the inevitable. The origin of the free delivery custom is easily traceable. Somewhere in New England or New York the manufacture of a certain article is begun. Profits are large, and a flourishing trade with the West is established. By and by new capital enters the field, and a manufactory of the same or a similar article is built further westward. In the struggle for control of the market it is clear that each must wholly relinquish all trade from points nearer to its rival than to itself, or must equalize freight rates. A New York manufacturer cannot sell his goods in Illinois in competition with those of Chicago make, unless he delivers them as cheaply in one city as in the other, and vice versa. The result is the establishment of a few prominent points for common delivery of articles made both in the East and the West, and St. Paul is such a point. Many of the most important lines of goods, articles that are staples of consumption throughout the Northwest, are delivered here to our jobbers at precisely the same figures charged a Chicago dealer. The Eastern jobber resents the apparent discrimination, but he is powerless to help himself. Neither can the manufacturer, who is forced to foot the bills or lose his custom. As one of his guild remarks in discussing this subject, which has been much agitated of late in some of the trade journals: "All that manufacturers can do is to make factories the points of delivery, except when manufacturers of the same or similar lines have advantage of location." When this happens they must equalize perforce by paying the freight balance themselves. It is now very clear why the jobbing trade is concentrating here. On all lines of goods where this manufacturers' competition exists, the cost price in St. Paul is identical with that in Chicago. Every man doing business in the Northwest and laying in his stock in Chicago, therefore, makes out of his profits a gift to the railroad company equal to the freight between Chicago and St. Paul. In other lines of articles not subject to this rule, we have already shown that this point can compete on more than equal terms with any Eastern market. Striking, then, an average of the whole, it is so apparent that the balance of power for the trade of the Northwest is on our side, that an Eastern manufacturer, in answer to urgent requests to favor the jobbers of his own section, replies: "The control of the jobbing trade of this country is bound to pass out of the grip of New York and other Eastern cities, just as rapidly as the West advances in population and enterprise."

STATISTICS OF THE WHOLESALE TRADE.

In reviewing the figures of St. Paul's wholesale trade for 1883, it must be borne in mind that the Northern Pacific railway was not completed in time to materially affect the volume of business; but that upon the driving of the last spike in September, 1883, an entirely new, rich and fairly populous field of trade was made directly tributary to this city — the territory of the mountains and the Pacific slope, with its half million people and endless variety of resources of wealth and future development. The completion of the Northern Pacific, indeed, added suddenly one-half to St. Paul's field of operations.

OFFICIAL FIGURES.

The following statistics of St. Paul's wholesale trade for 1883, have been secured direct from the yearly balance sheets of respective firms, by the Secretary of the Chamber of Commerce, and are therefore exact:

WHOLESALE BUSINESS COMPARED BY YEARS.

	1881	1882	1883
Number of establishments	223	276	325
Number of employees	3,189	4,684	5,815
Amount of sales	$46,355,999	$56,628,494	$72,048,771

The figures of the table indicate a remarkable steadiness of growth in the wholesale trade of the city, and prove beyond any question that notwithstanding the increase in new houses, all the old firms are constantly augmenting their annual sales. This latter statement is verified by the fact that the ratio of increased sales is much larger than the ratio of increased firms. It is also determined by the ratio of increased number of employees as compared with the number of new houses. There can be no clearer proof of the healthy condition of the wholesale business of St. Paul.

DETAILED STATISTICS OF THE BUSINESS OF 1883.

KIND OF BUSINESS.	No. of Establish- ments.	No. of Employees.	Amount of Sales — 1883.	Increase over 1882.
Agricultural implements	9	85	$2,163,800	$255,800
Beer	14	79	1,157,321	69,167
Blank books, paper and church goods	7	87	1,036,000	*200,036
Boots and shoes	5	90	2,910,000	85,000
Cigars and tobacco	18	52	1,267,000	616,700
Clothing	3	73	825,000	25,000
Coffees, teas, spices, etc	6	60	781,000	89,000
Confectionery, fruit and bakers' products	7	140	1,502,000	30,750
Crockery and glassware	3	57	479,000	5,000
Drugs, paints and oils	8	159	2,500,000	740,000
Dry goods, toys and notions	13	374	9,152,000	7,500
Fuel and pig iron	13	738	4,358,000	1,469,666
Furniture	9	83	533,000	78,000
Grain, flour, feed and commission	47	95	6,300,000	424,264
Groceries	11	428	13,287,000	*296,000
Guns and sporting goods	2	9	110,000	*40,000
Hardware, stoves and heavy iron	17	269	4,467,750	484,810
Hats, caps and furs	4	70	1,250,000	75,000
Hides and furs	6	47	716,600	*84,000
Jewelry	4	11	77,500	
Leather, saddlery and findings	7	90	981,000	349,374
Lime and cement	3	10	212,000	
Live stock	9	56	2,572,000	79,856
Lumber	17	1,620	3,660,000	226,378
Machinery and mill supplies	8	129	1,208,000	9,800
Millinery and lace goods	3	42	500,000	
Musical instruments	6	78	488,300	59,300
Printing material	3	13	181,000	
Provisions	7	89	1,313,000	112,000
Sash, doors and blinds	5	116	791,000	99,000
Trunks and valises	2	30	200,000	
Wines and liquors	14	88	2,060,000	*271,484
Miscellaneous	35	448	2,959,000	
Totals	325	5,815	$72,048,771	$5,385,365

* Decrease.

Miscellaneous includes bar supplies, billiard tables, brewers' supplies, bricks, brooms, brushes, carpets, fish, junk, ice, photographic materials, rubber goods, seeds, soap, steam heating, stoneware, surgical instruments, undertakers, upholstery, vinegar, wooden and willow ware, woolen and tailors' trimmings.

The apparent decrease in the volume of the grocery trade is easily explained, the figures representing gross value of sales and not amount of merchandise; and, as there was a heavy decline in prices during 1883, as compared with 1882, the volume of the grocery business appears to be $296,000 less, when in reality it was over 9 per cent greater in amount of goods sold; and on the basis of prices of 1882 the sales of 1883 would have aggregated $14,428,240 — or an increase of $1,191,240.

WHAT RECEIPTS OF CUSTOMS PROVE.

Proof of the growth of St. Paul's wholesale trade, is found in the official reports of the United States collector of customs for this district. There are now between fifty and sixty firms in this city that import largely; and it may be mentioned, incidentally, that all classes of foreign goods, brought in bond to St. Paul, can be sold throughout the Northwest for less money than those breaking bulk in New York or Chicago, and then refreighted to this region. The figures presented are from the official reports of the past five years. The business man not familiar with the growth of St. Paul's wholesale trade for the past few years, will read with some astonishment that the customs receipts at St. Paul have increased over 500 per cent since 1879, or within five years. By these figures, as in others presented

VIEW IN THE WHOLESALE DISTRICT.

Third Street Below Wisconsin

in this pamphlet, it will be seen that the beginning of St. Paul's phenomenal development, was in 1881; and that up to the present time the ratio of that development has constantly increased; proving, in fact, that the city's growth and prosperity has but just begun. It will be seen that the customs receipts from all sources for 1879, were but $11,821.56; that the receipts for 1881, were nearly three times as large as those of 1879; and that the receipts of 1883 were more than double those of 1881.

THE OFFICIAL FIGURES.

Year.	Amount.
1879	$11,821.56
1880	16,788.07
1881	30,800.85
1882	45,248.28
1883	64,016.06

LIST OF IMPORTERS.

The following is a list of St. Paul firms that imported largely during 1883. Among notable importations were 450,000 pounds of tea direct from Japan, and 13,911 bags of coffee from South America, by a single firm, the P. H. Kelly Mercantile company:

P. H. Kelly Mercantile Co.
Auerbach, Finch & Van Slyck.
Lindekes, Warner & Schurmeier.
Noyes Brothers & Cutler.
George Benz & Co.
B. Kuhl & Co.
Monfort & Co.
Hesse & Damcke.
C. Gotzian & Co.
Smith Brothers.
Joseph Masson.
A. Allen.
Beaupre, Keogh & Co.
Ranney & Hodgman.

T. M. Metcal..
Mannheimer Brothers.
Campbell & Burbank.
Conrad Schmidt.
Kennedy Brothers.
Craig, Larkin & Smith.
Perkins, Lyons & Co.
D. O'Halloran.
Dyer & Howard.
D. Aberle & Co.
William Theobald.
Lambie & Bethune.
Drake Brothers.
Merell, Sahlgaard & Thwing.

St. Paul Book & Stationery Co.
J. W. Donaldson.
Forepaugh & Tarbox.
Ward, Hill & McClellan.
Arthur, Warren & Abbott.
W. L. McGrath & Co.
George Palmes.
Duncan & Barry
Zimmerman Brothers.
Schultz, Becht & Hospes.
Allen, Moon & Co.
Hoxsie & Jaggar.
Glidden, Griggs & Co.
Schulze & Macdonald.

COMMERCIAL AGENCY FIGURES.

According to the reference books of Bradstreet's Commercial Agency, over six hundred new business (wholesale and retail,) concerns began operations in St. Paul during 1883. The agency of R. G. Dun & Co., places the number of new houses within two years at over 1,250, and gives the total number of St. Paul business firms in 1879 — only four years ago — at five hundred and seventy. For two years past St. Paul has therefore added each year to its trade capacity, more business houses than it had in 1879. The total number of business firms in the city at this time, is between two and three thousand. Of 1,669 houses, Dun & Co. fix responsibility as follows, showing the aggregate capital of St. Paul business concerns to be not far from $75,000,000:

5 houses, responsibility over				$1,000,000	$5,000,000
6	"	"	"	750,000	4,500,000
17	"	"	"	500,000	8,500,000
33	"	"	"	300,000	9,900,000
51	"	"	"	200,000	10,200,000
70	"	"	"	125,000	8,750,000
107	"	"	"	75,000	8,025,000
162	"	"	"	40,000	6,480,000
268	"	"	"	20,000	5,360,000
105	"	"	"	10,000	4,050,000
545	"	"	"	5,000	2,725,000
					$73,490,000

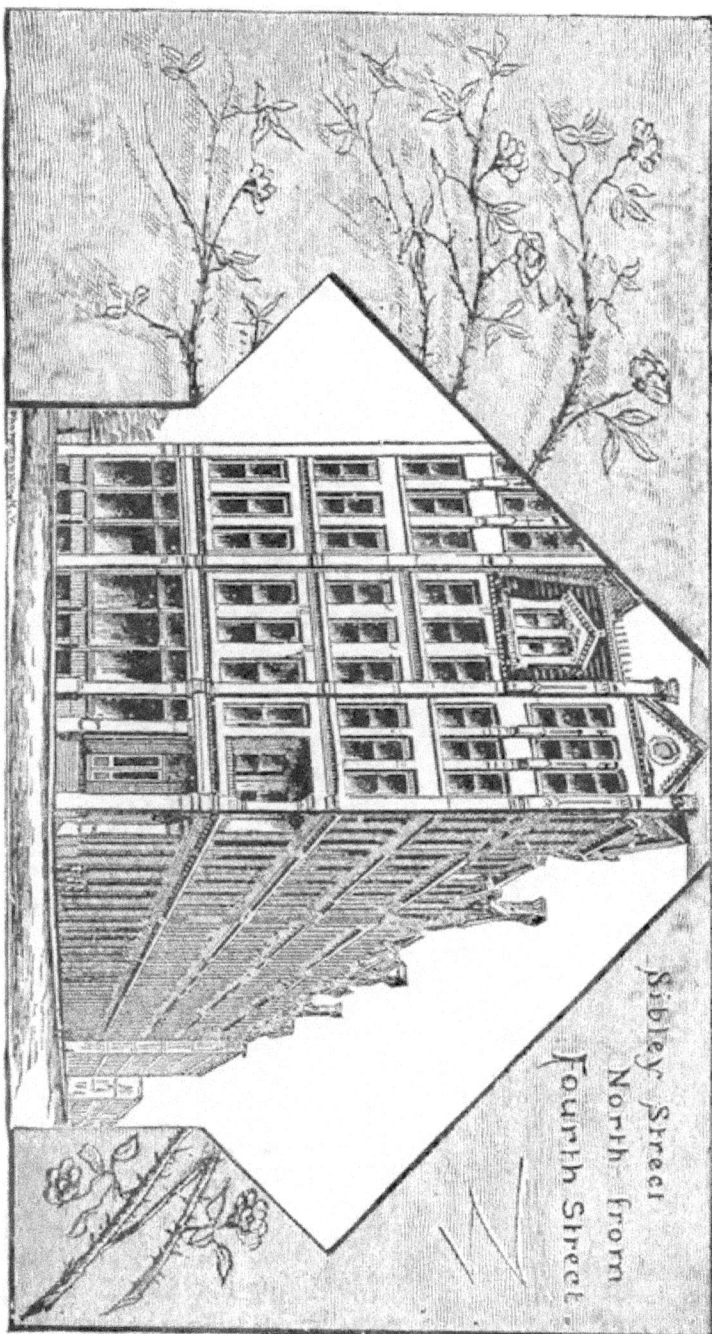

VIEW IN THE WHOLESALE DISTRICT.

Sibley Street
North from
Fourth Street.

AN UNEQUALED RECORD.

There remains to be added a very important official statement with reference to the wholesale trade of St. Paul, and one which the business world will thoroughly appreciate. The announcement is on the authority of Bradstreet, and is that not a single failure has occurred among St. Paul wholesale houses within three years. This, in view of the business troubles of the past two years, is a remarkable showing. Not only has there been no failures in the time specified, but Bradstreet goes further and rates the established houses as exceedingly prosperous. It is hardly necessary to add that no Western or Northwestern city, save St. Paul, can report officially that its wholesale trade has sustained no failure since 1880.

A FUTURE TEA MARKET.

Since the opening of the Northern Pacific railway, St. Paul has become an important tea market, and dealers here predict that this city will speedily become the principal distributing point for the chief products of China and Japan. Although the railway was not completed in time to permit of a fair showing in this line for the year 1883, the official figures show that St. Paul merchants imported over half a million pounds of tea direct from China and Japan within three months from the time the Northern Pacific was opened to through traffic. St. Paul is certain to become one of the great primary tea markets of America, if not the largest on the continent. The same may be said with reference to all the products imported into this country via the Pacific.

Great and prosperous as St. Paul's wholesale trade has now become, as indicated by the figures given, it bids fair to be even more prosperous, and increase more rapidly during the next few years than it has at any in the past. The rapid concentration of railways at this point affords all the evidence that is needed on that score.

ROOM FOR NEW CONCERNS.

While the above tabulated statements may be of slight interest to the general reader, the business man looking toward the Northwest for a favorable opportunity to locate, will be especially interested in the details given ; for they will show him just what lines occupy the field at present, to what extent, and what the average business of each concern probably is. By careful study of the figures presented he will be convinced that no branch of wholesaling or jobbing is as yet overdone in St. Paul. The Northwestern domain is developing, in fact, much more rapidly than wholesale houses are increasing in this city.

The Retail Trade.

Every business man is aware that retailers are particularly prosperous in rapidly growing cities. This fact accounts, perhaps, for the remarkable absence of failures among St. Paul concerns. In this latter respect no other city of like population and number of establishments can show so clean a record for the past five years. An examination of Bradstreet's reports affords the best possible proof of the general prosperity of St. Paul retailers, for it shows that the rating of the general average of firms is increased year by year. This, of course means much to the business man — far more than any possible argument supported by mere trade statistics. A single, but by no means exceptional case, which was noted while vari-

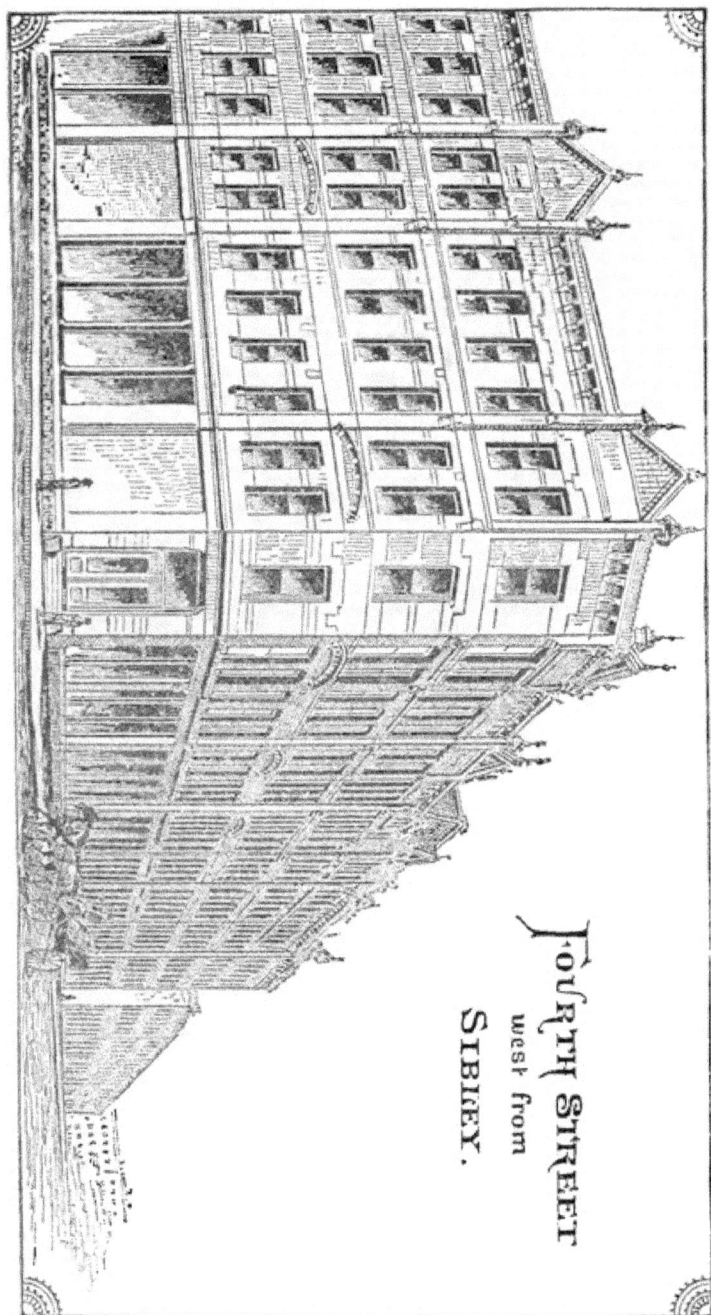

VIEW IN THE WHOLESALE DISTRICT.

FOURTH STREET west from SIBLEY.

ous statistics were being secured from Bradstreet's reports, was of a retailer in an ordinary line who started here in 1881 with a rating of $5,000. In 1882, he was rated $10,000, and is now given $35,000. These are actual figures from official sources, and are given to illustrate what seem to be a regular yearly increase in the rating of the majority of St. Paul retailers. To show that business is not overdone in this city it should be stated that the per cent of increase yearly in retail establishments is not above one-half the increase in population. The following statistics will show that the number of retail houses is really small in proportion to the 100,000 population of the city. In the leading lines the number of houses worthy of note are:

Kind of Business.	No.	Kind of Business.	No.
Dry goods	22	Livery stables	21
Groceries	153	Millinery	23
Hardware	35	Clothing	30
Furnishing goods, hats, etc.	31	Cigars and tobacco	63
Boots and shoes	33	Bakeries	19
Meat markets	52	Books and stationery	15
Merchant tailors	31	Carpets	7
Furs, etc.	29	Confectionery	39
Produce	11	Furniture	23
Crockery and glassware	8	Lumber dealers	23
Drugs	35	Second hand goods	10
Fancy goods	16	Jewelry	20
Fruits, etc.	17	Wood and Coal	16

The professions are largely represented by young men, all of whom seem to meet with success.

In selecting a location for retail establishments, in choosing a future field for professional life, or in looking for a place to ply any honest trade, the reader cannot afford to ignore the opportunities offered in St. Paul.

St. Paul's Manufactures.

The total value of the products of St. Paul's manufactures in 1870 was but a little over $1,000,000, and less than 1,000 persons, all told, were afforded employment in the industrial establishments of the city. At this time it was beginning to be evident that the town would soon become a railway and commercial center, and the idea once seized upon it grew at home and abroad until it completely overshadowed all thought or talk of the possibilties of the young metropolis as a manufacturing place. Indeed, the general rule was to disclaim importance for St. Paul in the industrial line. In the meantime Art and Science, always less obtrusive than Commerce and Finance, builded more rapidly and extensively than was publicly appreciated, until now the official figures prove that manufactures have really kept pace with every other feature of development. The subjoined tabulated reports show that the manufactures of St. Paul have increased from 88 establishments in 1870, employing 985 persons and aggregating $1,611,378 value of products, to 758 establishments in 1883, with 13,979 employees and $25,885,471 value of products. The tables will also indicate that this growth to greatness has been remarkably steady and persistent, and that St. Paul cannot fail to become the future seat of manufactures while it is becoming the metropolis of the Northwest in other respects. The statistics given are the best possible proof that shrewd manufacturers no longer regard cheap motive power (water) as an essential in the question of location, compared with railway, financial and market facilities afforded; and just

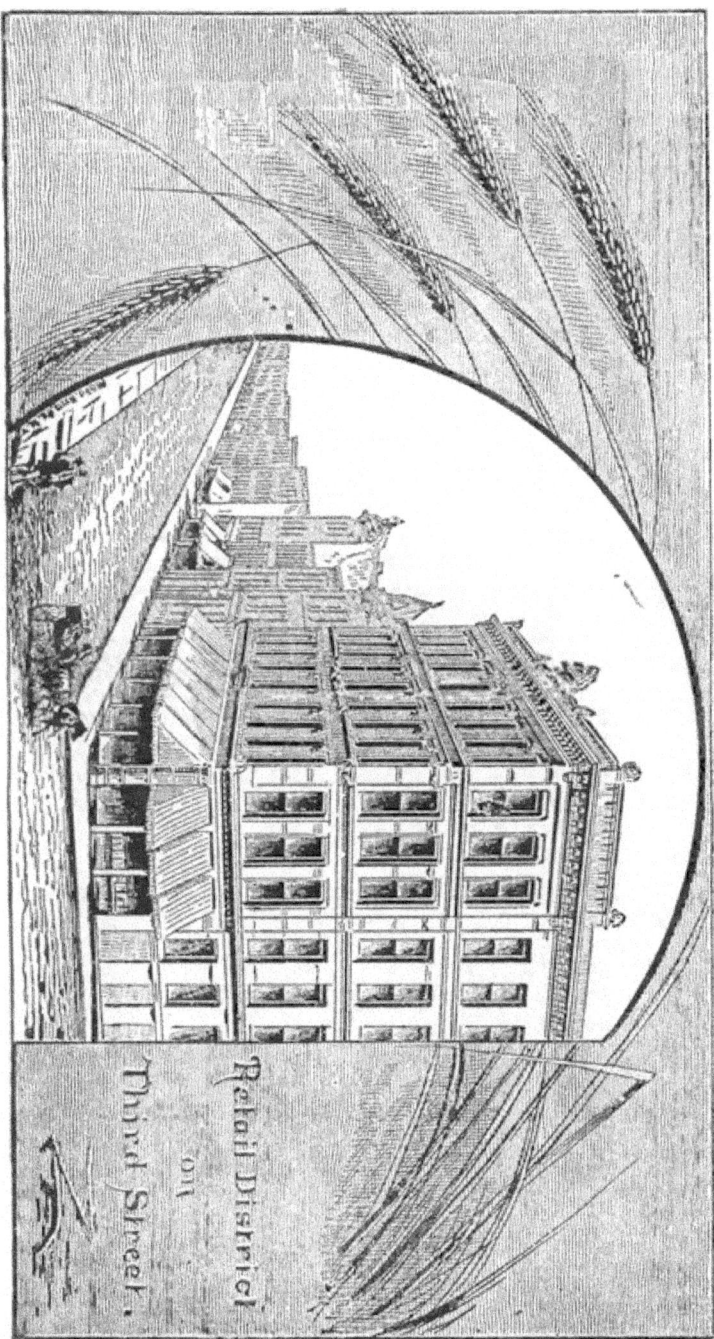

VIEW IN THE RETAIL DISTRICT.

Retail District
on
Third Street.

in proportion as this city waxes strong in these latter respects, so will manufactures increase and thrive.   Not less than 64 new, and mostly important, manufacturing enterprises were established during 1883.

DETAILED STATISTICS OF MANUFACTURES.

YEAR.	No. Estab-lishments.	No. Employees.	Value of Products.
1870	88	985	$1,611,378
1874	216	2,155	3,953,000
1878	332	3,117	6,150,000
1880	542	6,629	11,806,824
1881	667	8,188	15,466,201
1882	694	12,267	22,390,589
1883	758	13,979	25,885,471

THE WORK OF 1883.

KIND OF BUSINESS.	No. of Establish-ments.	No. of em-ployees.	Value of prod-uct—1883.	Increase over 1882.
Agricultural implements	2	295	$800,000	*$64,000
Blacksmiths and wheelwrights	16	75	56,000	9,100
Bookbinding	7	89	90,000	4,146
Boots and shoes	25	407	1,025,000	196,123
Brewers, maltsters and bottlers	13	193	914,623	106,367
Bricks and tiles	12	250	170,000	11,100
Brooms and brushes	6	42	55,500	250
Cigars	32	492	800,000	28,000
Clothing	78	1,500	2,300,000	518,834
Coffees, spices and baking powder	6	120	795,000	1,896
Confectionery	9	83	275,000	9,000
Contractors and builders	147	3,921	4,947,000	787,140
Crackers and bakery products	28	300	1,000,000	199,500
Drugs, chemicals and oils	6	50	405,000	76,160
Flour and grist milling	7	85	1,560,000	113,000
Furniture and upholstery	24	275	560,000	56,000
Furs	7	172	426,000	263,700
Harness and saddlery	13	133	300,000	73,067
Iron, architectural	3	132	265,000	155,550
Jewelry and watchmaking	7	33	32,400	34,000
Machine shops, foundries and boiler works	16	422	745,000	98,640
Marble and stone cutting	20	94	176,000	54,000
Millinery, lace and fancy goods	20		97,000	9,670
Painting and glazing	12	121	225,000	3,360
Photography	13	39	63,000	
Pictures and frames	4	17	25,000	
Printing and publishing	43	1,120	1,698,000	293,520
Railroad repairs and car making	4	1,385	1,417,148	71,939
Sash, doors, boxes and planing mills	8	400	484,000	*15,500
Slaughtering and meat packing	60	250	1,675,000	235,000
Tin and hardware, stoves and plumbing	15	139	450,000	232,186
Trunks and valises	2	92	120,000	*30,000
Wagons and carriages	22	313	612,000	18,000
Miscellaneous	61	510	1,301,800	215,400
Total	758	13,979	$25,885,471	$3,811,482

* Decrease.

Miscellaneous includes awnings and tents, bleachers, boats, brass works, carpet weavers, carriage trimmers, cooperage, cutlery grinding, dyeing, engraving, fire-proof building material, fire works, hair goods, hoop and skirt factory, knit goods, lighting companies, mineral waters, musical instruments, opticians, rendering companies, renovator of cloth, sewer and drain pipes, shingle bands, shoe cases, soap, sporting goods, stamps and seals, steam heating, taxidermist, terra cotta, type foundry, vinegar and catsup, wire works,

The manufacturer who scans the statistics above given will quickly discover some, at least, of the many rare openings offered in St. Paul. In the succeeding chapter will be found "hints to manufacturers," wherein opportunities are discussed at greater length and more specifically.

"Union Block," represented above, is 101 feet 6 inches front by 140 feet deep. It has been carefully constructed, and is one of the finest as well as most costly blocks in the city. It is designed for stores and offices and has headquarters for manufacturers' and jobbers' agents, several large and well-lighted apartments having been planned expressly for their accommodation. It is owned by Commodore Wm. F. Davidson and Colonel James H. Davidson of St. Paul, and is valued with the ground at $250,000. Its rentals aggregate between $25,000 and $30,000.

Hints to Manufacturers.

Manufacturers disregard nowadays traditions which once assigned them exclusively to sites upon water-powers, and seek commercial and financial centers; this with the knowledge that economic motive power *per se* cannot compensate for location apart from general business and railway facilities. Chicago presents the latest and best illustration of this fact, although St. Louis and Philadelphia afford evidence to the same effect. Even as the first named city offered, a score or more of years ago, the greatest possible inducements for the establishment of varied manufacturing industries—because of its position as the commercial depot of the West and Northwest—so does St. Paul at this time present precisely similar opportunities. The arguments (presented elsewhere in detail) which go to prove the certainty of St. Paul's future development and importance, are sufficient to convince the manufacturer that this is the site above all others for the location of any industry, the product of which is to seek sale among and patronage from the people of the Upper Mississippi valley, and the country west and northwest to the Pacific coast.

It must be borne constantly in mind by the manufacturer who is now looking toward St. Paul as a favorable site for this or that industrial enterprise, that the chief merit of the selection does not exist in securing an unoccupied field with the certainty of fair immediate returns—a good enough inducement in itself, one would say—but is due to the opportunity to develop capacity and production in the line operated, in proportion as the country tributary to St. Paul becomes populous. It must be kept in view that the empire of the Northwest—aggregating the most fertile agricultural lands, the most extensive cattle ranges, the richest mineral region and the most valuable and extensive forests of the entire country—is equal in area to more than one quarter of the United States and that it is developing more rapidly at this time than any other region on the continent has developed in the past. It must also be remembered that by reason of its railway facilities St. Paul is the natural market of all this territory; that the Northern Pacific—with its headquarters and principal terminus here—is a main highway of all the region indicated, and the only and controlling route of trade and commerce for the greater portion of the entire area. The manufacturer, then, who locates in St. Paul is not dependent upon present trade conditions, favorable as they may seem, but is merely starting a plant that cannot but expand year by year as the country tributary grows in wealth, population and necessities. What Chicago is to-day as a manufacturing center, St. Paul, backed by its commercial, transportation and financial facilities, and the natural resources of the country tributary and accessible, will be within a very few years; and the time is not far distant when this city will rival in this regard every manufacturing place in the valley of the Mississippi.

THE FUEL SUPPLY.

Many Eastern manufacturers have an erroneous opinion concerning the matter of fuel supply in this locality, believing that works requiring constant and heavy consumption of coal or coke cannot be profitably operated here. So far as the best anthracite coal and coke is concerned, it costs more to place it in St. Paul, of course, than it does in Pittsburg and many other Eastern manufacturing centers. But this excess in cost of these particular fuels to St. Paul is more than counterbalanced by the accessibility of St. Paul to the most extensive copper mines in

Gilfillan Block, corner Fourth and Jackson.—Bank and general office building.—Aggregate rentals, $25,000 per annum

the world and to the largest and most valuable iron mines in the country; for before the close of the present year St. Paul will have more direct and cheaper access to first-class Bessemer ores than Pittsburg ever had. Then, too, St. Paul can secure anthracite coal and coke by way of the lakes to Duluth, and thence 150 miles only by rail, at much less cost of freightage than the heavy manufactured goods can be shipped to this point, to say nothing about the shipping of the heavy ores from the Peninsula of Michigan to Eastern manufactories. Again, St. Paul is not compelled to depend upon the coal fields of Pennsylvania, for it has near and cheap access to the immense coal fields of Iowa, not to mention those of Illinois, which may be reached by cheap river freightage. In fact, coal and coke of any variety can be delivered in St. Paul at the present time within a small per cent of the cost of delivery in Chicago. So far as charcoal is concerned, it can be furnished in St. Paul at far less cost than it can possibly be obtained in Chicago or Cleveland. In addition to these facts, St. Paul will soon be able, if necessary, to procure coal from the West, where immense deposits exist in Dakota and Montana. In wood supply, St. Paul can boast of unlimited quantity at lower prices than any Eastern manufacturing city can now secure. Averaging cost, and St. Paul can secure wood, charcoal and soft coal at lower prices than Chicago can.

IRON AND STEEL WORKS.

Pittsburg, Cleveland and Chicago iron workers will doubtless be surprised to learn that so far as nearness to first-class Bessemer ores is concerned, St. Paul actually has a decided advantage over either of the great iron and steel marts named, yet the statement is true, and in the proof here afforded may be information of greatest value to those directly interested. It is well known, of course, that Pittsburg is compelled, by reason of the inferior quality of its local ores, to combine many different mine products together—even securing ores for admixture from Missouri and Tennessee—in order to produce first-class results. Cleveland is dependent entirely upon the mines of the Peninsula of Michigan, while Chicago draws her supply from the same source. Cleveland and Chicago are compelled to use a combination of both rail and water routes in securing their iron ores, or else all rail, as Chicago sometimes does, via the Northwestern railroad from the Peninsula mines. The fact that Chicago does receive some of its ores via all rail proves that the iron makers there can afford to haul first-class ores a distance of over 400 miles. Now, the distance from these very mines by rail to St. Paul will be but 330 miles when the St. Paul Eastern Grand Trunk is completed to Wausau, on the Wisconsin river, or less than 300 miles when the Sault Ste. Marie railway is built through to the Michigan peninsula. But St. Paul has a far better showing to make in this regard. Undoubtedly the largest and best deposits of specular hematite ores (the true Bessemer ores) on the American continent are now being developed in the State of Minnesota, in what is known as the Vermillion Lake district, 260 miles nearly due north from St. Paul. The value of these mines is more conclusively and clearly demonstrated by the character of the men engaged in their development than by any paid-for analyses; and it is sufficient to state that the Towers of Pennsylvania, the Elys of Cleveland and Breitung of Michigan are the iron men who have organized the company which is now spending $4,000,000 in building the Duluth & Iron Range railway through the heart of an absolute wilderness of forest, rock and swamp, in order to make this greatest iron discovery of the age accessible. And it should also be remembered that Cleveland and Chicago iron workers expect to utilize to advantage the Vermillion ores, which are but 200 miles from St. Paul, and which will be accessible from this city before the close of the present season. In addition to the above unsurpassed resources of raw material, St. Paul capital is now developing what promises to be an excellent and inexhaustible supply of iron ore at Black River Falls, Wis., 165 miles by rail from this city; preparations for the building of a blast furnace at that point being now under way. With these advantages in favor of St. Paul, it is undoubtedly the best point in the United States to locate first-class iron and steel works. The time has come, indeed, either for the establishment of vast works that will have capacity to manufacture merchant iron and steel, rails, nails, all kinds of agricultural tools, fine-edged tools, saws, mill machinery, etc., etc., or else for works that can furnish the iron and steel for concerns that may make specialties of any of the lines above indicated. With so vast a field for all kinds of iron and steel goods and machinery as the Northwest will soon present, works of the character specified are imperative. That they would be profitable from the very start there is no doubt. So far as various requisites of fuel are concerned, it is self-evident that it is cheaper to bring light coke from the East (and we shall soon have it from the West) than it is to transport iron ores to Cleveland, Chicago, etc., and freight back the heavy manufactured products. St. Paul, by reason of its nearness to the best iron ores of the country, certainly has decided advantage over places like Cleveland, Erie, etc., where iron and steel works are the principal manufactures. A chief advantage of works located in St. Paul would be their proximity to an exclusive market, which is growing greater and greater with marvelous rapidity. Of course it is only a question of brief time when iron and steel works of magnitude will be established in this city, and the manufacturers in this line who will investigate now and locate quickly will be the ones to profit most by the unparalleled opportunities here offered.

TANNERIES.

By virtue of favorable conditions, St. Paul should, ere this, have become an important tanning center; yet its almost incomparable resources and facilities in this direction seem to have been entirely overlooked. It is indeed strange that this city should be the chief market of the countless hides produced annually in the Northwest, be situated at the western door, so to speak, of the vast hemlock forests of Wisconsin, and yet secure its leather from localities not nearly so well adapted to its manufacture. The general situation may be most easily explained by comparisons. Take Milwaukee, for instance, which is now one of the great tanning centers of the country: It secures its bark by ship load from the Michigan or Green Bay pineries, or by rail from the Wisconsin pineries; its hides—a majority of them—pass through St. Paul from various gathering depots throughout the Northwest; the manufactured products find market in the very region from whence its supply of raw material was drawn. In other words, Milwaukee is able to gather many of its hides in, around and beyond St. Paul, and returns its leather to the same region at a profit. St. Paul is nearer to both bark and hides supplies than is Milwaukee, has equal or better facilities for obtaining them, and would be a better market for the manufactured product. It also has equal, if not better, water facilities. What, then, is to hinder profitable return for investment in this line? In this connection the practical tanner will also realize that the present source of bark supply to Milwaukee and Chicago by water communication is getting pretty well exhausted, and that in the near future those great tanning centers must seek their hemlock by rail at a distance of between two and three hundred miles, from the very district near at hand to St. Paul, Northern Wisconsin, and which is all the time being brought into closer and closer communication with this city. It will also be realized that in the rapid development of the Northwest, its hide product must vastly increase, and that so great a volume of raw material or resource cannot long flow past unheeded. Then, again, as the country develops, so increases the demand for the manufactured product; and it only remains for those practical manufacturers who now seize upon the opportunities here offered, to reap the first and best fruits of that which is certain to become—and within a very few years—a leading industry in St. Paul. To summarize: Bark and hides may be placed in St. Paul at less cost than in either Chicago or Milwaukee; the ratio of saving in favor of St. Paul will increase annually; St. Paul's market is the entire Northwest, the needs of which for the manufactured product will keep pace with its constantly increasing ability to furnish raw material.

CANNED GOODS.

Southern and Eastern people, visiting St. Paul for the first time, and noting perchance the stocks in mercantile establishments, are invariably surprised at the quantity of canned goods displayed for sale. Wholesale houses import this class of goods not only by tons, but by car lots, and the annual aggregate is represented in money value by hundreds upon hundreds of thousand dollars. The market is not restricted to the lumber and mining camps, that of course consume great quantities, but is general among all classes of people, owing to the long winter season when canned vegetables and fruits must take the place of "early garden truck" procurable in Southern localities. The largest invoices of this class are of sweet corn and tomatoes, and in these, too, are said to be largest profits. It so happens that the latitude and locality of St. Paul is particularly favorable to the growth of both sweet corn and tomatoes. It is a recognized fact these two garden products attain their best quality where their growth to maturity is most rapid ; and in this is the secret of their pronounced success in this vicinity. Sweet corn, especially, is grown here to a degree of perfection seldom or never attained in more southern latitudes. The sun is hot while it is hot, and therefore both sweet corn and tomatoes flourish to the very best advantage during their season ; in fact, small fruits and vegetables thrive as well as in any portion of the country, and most kinds acquire perfection of flavor not to be met with elsewhere. While the soil and climate are eminently fitted to produce the products necessary to profitable canning, and while here is the largest market for canned goods on the continent, yet there is no industry of the kind in St. Paul or vicinity. It is doubtful if any new enterprise would be more successful in St. Paul than an establishment for canning small fruits and vegetables, especially sweet corn and tomatoes. The field is open, and particularly inviting.

REDUCTION WORKS.

Works for the reduction of silver and copper ores have been successfully established and conducted in Omaha and Denver in the West, and in several New Jersey towns, Baltimore, etc., in the East. Within the past few months, thousands of tons of silver ores have been transported from Montana and other far Western mines, via the Northern Pacific and St. Paul, to New Jersey, for reduction. Even at so great a disadvantage in length of haul and cost of freightage, the experiment has proved profitable to miners and reducers. Such being the case, it is very evident that reduction works in St. Paul would be bonanzas of profit to investors in plants of that character. Reduction works, like physicians and lawyers, may count upon business in direct ratio as their reputation for intelligent and honest service is acknowledged ; the miner feeling assured that it pays better to send his ores to the far East, if thereby he may secure skillful treatment of them and honest returns, than to trust to crude or extravagant methods often employed nearer the scenes of his labor. It is stated on the authority of Montana miners themselves that if reduction works of the first class were established by capitalists of reputation in St. Paul, that there would never be cause to close them through lack of patronage. Not only would St. Paul be able to displace Eastern works in handling silver ores, but would certainly be able to compete with Chicago, or any other point, in reducing the copper and silver ores from Lake Superior. Within less than eighteen months, at the farthest, St. Paul will be in closer and more direct rail communication with the copper mines of Northern Michigan than Chicago now is. The silver mines of the north-shore of Lake Superior are daily coming into more and more prominence, and will soon afford revenue to reduction works. So far as coke is concerned, it may certainly be brought to St. Paul at much less proportionate expense than heavy ores can be freighted to the East. The completion of the Northern Pacific railway, and the consequent investigation

THE ST. PAUL MARKET HOUSE, CORNER OF SEVENTH AND WABASHA STREETS.

of the mineral regions through which it runs, is bringing to light the inexhaustible mineral resources of the country between the Rocky mountains and the Pacific, and is affording daily proof that successful prospecting in Montana, Wyoming, Idaho and Washington Territories has but just begun. No point in the United States to-day offers so splendid an opening for reduction works as is presented by St. Paul.

BREWERIES AND DISTILLERIES.

As a rule the makers of malt liquors and high wines are quick to discover productive and favorable fields for their operations; yet the inducements offered for manufacture at this point have been in great part overlooked. The brewers of Wisconsin and Illinois find a large and constantly increasing market for their goods in the Northwest, and show by the maintenance of numerous agencies that they can afford to buy barley in St. Paul, transport it to Milwaukee and Chicago, pay excessive inspection and storage charges thereon, manufacture beer and return it to all Northwestern points to be sold on draught or in bottles. St. Paul offers certain advantages to brewers that neither Milwaukee nor Chicago can approach: First is the matter of grain supply, whether the barley is procured from the Northwest or the Pacific slope; second is the ease of securing ice (one of the most important factors), in which regard Chicago and Milwaukee are placed at very great disadvantage; third may be mentioned the unequaled sites offered by the bluffs about the city which may cheaply be excavated (the bluffs are composed of soft sand rock) for great cooling and torage cellars; and the fourth consideration is the extent of country to be supplied from this point.

Distilleries located in St. Paul would secure all the cattle they could feed every month of the year—one of the most important considerations in selecting a site for a distillery. The advantage in securing rye would offset the disadvantage in procuring corn, and the extent of market would more than compensate for the supposed advantages of more southern localities.

PACKING HOUSES.

St. Paul, so far as location is concerned, occupies the same position with reference to the Montana cattle trade that Kansas City does to the exportation of Texan beeves. It must be considered, however, that the vast ranges of Montana are rapidly supplanting, in both American and European markets, the meat products of Texas, because of the marked superiority of the Northern over the Southern fed and bred cattle. It is now conceded that the future beef product of America will be most largely furnished by Montana; and over eighty per cent of that product will always pass through St. Paul on its way to the markets of the world. At present the countless herds of Montana are shipped through St. Paul by rail to the great packing houses of Chicago and other Eastern and Southern cities—every hoof, every hide, every horn and the fifty per cent of offal paying heavy tribute in freightage. St. Paul, by reason of its being the terminus of the Northern Pacific railway—over the lines of which the Montana cattle must be shipped—and the railway radius for all lines to the South and East, should become the packing center for this vast and increasing product. If Chicago and Kansas City can profitably ship fresh meats by refrigerator cars to Eastern markets, when their ice costs at least one-fifth as much as their meat, how much more profitably might the same business be conducted in St. Paul, where there is no limit to the ice crop? Indeed, St. Paul is by location and in fact the distributing point for Montana cattle, and there is every possible advantage offered to the establishment of packing houses at this point. In addition to the Eastern market for boxed meats, there is a very large local demand—directly upon St. Paul—all through the pineries of Wisconsin and Minnesota. While beef-packing will always be the most important feature of houses that may be established in St. Paul, there is a considerable and rapidly increasing hog product throughout the Northwest. In the establishment of packing houses, St. Paul offers inducements to capitalists that no other city on the continent can equal.

Granite-faced block in the wholesale district at the northwest corner of Third and Sibley streets.

STOVE WORKS.

Extensive stove works seem to flourish in scores of towns like Detroit, Buffalo, Rochester, Cleveland, Milwaukee, etc., etc., where it would seem as though their patronage — so great is the competition — must necessarily be limited; yet all thrive abundantly. St. Paul, with its area of patronage the empire of the Northwest, offers special attractions to the manufacturer of stoves, furnaces, radiators, etc. Heating apparatus may be ranked almost first on the list of family requirements in this region, yet Eastern manufacturers have this great field practically to themselves. Stove works equal to the largest in the country would undoubtedly be taxed to their utmost capacity, if located in St. Paul, to meet even the local demand. In the matter of securing scrap and broken iron, stove works operated here would find great advantage over those of Eastern towns, for up to the present time old iron is a drug and nuisance, not only in St. Paul but all through the Northwest. With the opening of the iron mines at Black River Falls, Wis.,—now in process — pig iron may be secured near at hand (about 165 miles by rail), and the development of the Vermillion iron mines will place the best ores in the country within 200 miles of this city. If stove works are profitable in Detroit, Cleveland, etc., they certainly would be equally-as profitable (probably much more so) in St. Paul.

CLOTHING.

Inhabitants of a new country patronize the ready-made clothing merchant. Probably more goods, proportionately, of this class are sold in the lumber regions of Wisconsin and Minnesota, the agricultural towns of the Northwest and the cattle ranges and mining camps of the West, than in any like area of the United States. While there are large clothing-manufacturing concerns in St. Paul, their capacity is hardly a tithe of the requirements in this line of the wholesale market. The evident prosperity of the establishments now operated here is evidence enough that there is room for many others. Concerns located here would have that advantage over Chicago which personal and actual occupancy gives in any field of trade or enterprise.

CORDAGE WORKS.

Flax and hemp thrive as well in Minnesota as in any State in the Union, and the first named is already an important crop; but the field of rope and twine making is unoccupied. St. Paul presents an unusually favorable opportunity for the establishment of cordage works. The raw material might be developed easily and cheaply, and the market is not only the ordinary demand of every civilized community, but is enhanced by every bundle of grain grown on the Northwestern prairies, and cut by the harvesting machines which use twine in tying. The amount of twine used annually in Minnesota and Dakota in the harvest fields alone could not be supplied by any one cordage plant of ordinary capacity. The field of demand for the products of this industry is unlimited.

GLASS WORKS.

There are no glass works in St. Paul. Glass manufactured here would have in its favor, as compared with the Chicago market, 17 per cent of gross value; that amount being the estimate of St. Paul wholesalers for freight and breakage. Up to the present time no sand perfectly adapted to glass making has been discovered within the city limits, although it is very likely that no thorough search for it has ever been made. Every resident of St. Paul has remarked, however, the beautiful white sand rock so plentiful here. This sand is of precisely the right kind for glass making only that so far as tested it has proved too fine to melt properly — caking in the pots. The white sand is free from iron and would be faultless if it was but a trifle coarser. It is altogether probable that where such immense deposits of sand rock exist a little investigation would discover beds of coarser material than that which is now common, so fine, so much admired for its whiteness and fineness — and yet so useless. Tunnel City (about 160 miles) in Wisconsin, is as near to St. Paul as it is to other localities that use the sand found at that place, and so the inference may be drawn that glass works would pay in St. Paul, even if the sand used was brought from Tunnel City. In this connection it should be stated that a number of years ago a sample of sand was sent from this city to Eastern glass works and there tested and pronounced first-class, but the exact locality from which that sand was taken is not now known.

KNITTING WORKS.

Knitting works established in St. Paul within a year have been compelled to increase their capacity and general facilities. One establishment is doing its best, but it cannot hope to cope with the present, to say nothing of the future, demand upon the St. Paul market. For manufacturers with small capital there is a fine opening in this line. Heavy knitted goods are a great and growing requirement, and there is no danger of overstocking or of injurious competition. The lumber and mining camps consume great quantities of these goods, and the field is practically unlimited.

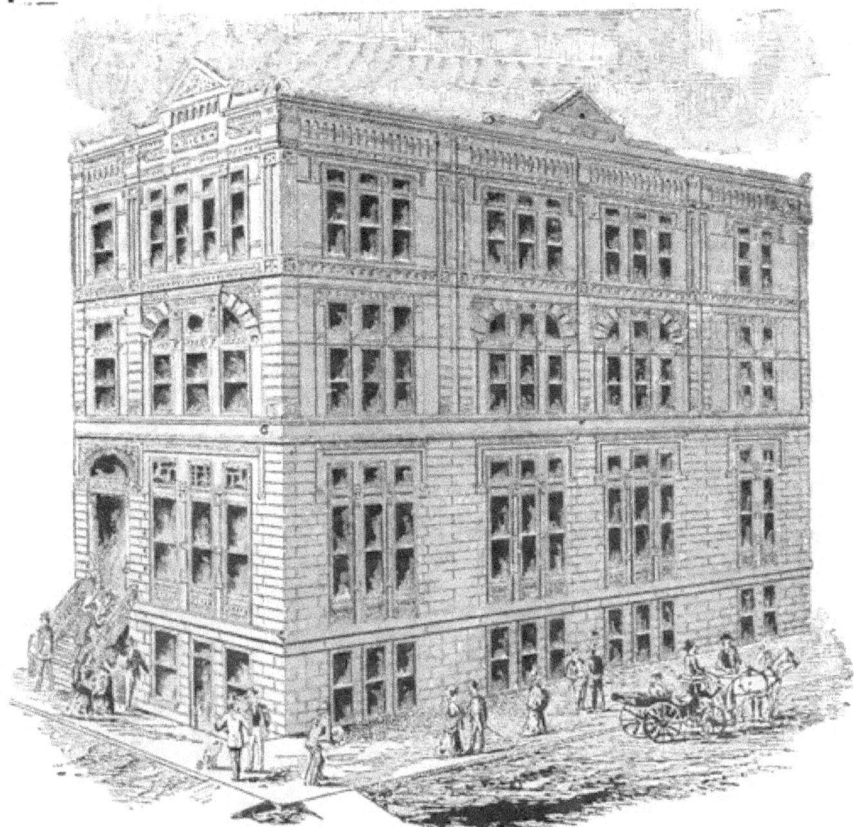

RICE BLOCK, CORNER FIFTH AND JACKSON.

WOOLEN GOODS.

The countless fleeces of Montana, the most rapidly-developing sheep range in America, should not be compelled to seek an Eastern market exclusively. If woolen mills can be successfully operated in Wisconsin towns, as they now are. they would certainly prove profitable in St. Paul, where they would be nearer to both the raw material and the market for the manufactured goods. There are several sites particularly fitted to woolen mill purposes that cannot, in growing St. Paul, long remain unutilized.

BOOTS AND SHOES.

The value of boots and shoes manufactured in St. Paul during 1883 was about one million dollars, while the wholesale trade in the same line reached three millions. The manufactories now established here are evidently prosperous. and the statistics given indicate that there is still room for concerns of this class on the present basis of trade, to say nothing of the future growth of the Northwestern demand. There is every certainty that additional boot and shoe factories may be established here and step at once into a lucrative permanent trade.

TOYS AND HOLIDAY GOODS.

Christmas comes as often in the Northwest as elsewhere, and owing to the general prosperity of the people and their well-known characteristic of spending money liberally if not lavishly, the holiday season at St. Paul and all tributary points is made much more of than in localities farther east where there is less youthful blood astir in the depths of winter. The result is an invariably large holiday trade. A house devoted exclusively to the manufacture of toys would undoubtedly secure immense patronage, as it would enable all local dealers to order more in accordance with their positive needs than they are now able to do while compelled to patronize Eastern factories and lay in large stocks or else run the risk of failing to meet the requirements of their trade ; making the local business somewhat hazardous.

WOODEN WARE.

Basswood, ash, Norway pine, willow and other woods required in the manufacture of wooden ware are easily and cheaply obtained in St. Paul. There is a boundless prairie country tributary to supply, and wherein wooden ware factories can never exist. St. Paul is, in fact, on the western edge of the timber belt which must in the future furnish the Northwest with its wooden ware. Now is the favorable time and opportunity for manufacturers of this class to investigate the opening offered here. Inasmuch as agricultural communities are the largest patrons of wooden ware, it may be said that the field to supply from this point is practically unlimited.

MATCH FACTORY.

There is an exceptional opportunity offered here for the establishment of a match factory. The field is entirely unoccupied and consists of the whole Northwest. Materials are cheaply procured. It requires but small capital to engage profitably in the manufacture of matches, and surely no other locality can offer equal inducements with those now held out by St. Paul.

FURNITURE.

The forests of Wisconsin and Minnesota, near at hand to St. Paul, supply abundance of butternut, birds-eye maple, basswood, ash, several varieties of oak, cherry and other kinds of cabinet woods, and Minnesota furnishes considerable black walnut. St. Paul is, therefore, an advantageous place for the establishment of furniture factories.

STARCH FACTORIES.

Potatoes are among the principal agricultural products of the Northwest, hence the chief requisite for starch factories is cheaply and easily obtained here. Starch works would undoubtedly pay a large profit on small investment.

BUILDING PAPER.

All through the Northwest building paper enters into the construction of houses. Tons upon tons are used in every town, village and city, and there is a constantly increasing market. The raw materials, straw, rags, etc., are more cheaply obtained here than at any point farther east, and an industry of this sort established in St. Paul would surely pay largely. Capital invested in this line would be certain of ample returns, and would build up an industry of magnitude.

BEET SUGAR INDUSTRY.

Experts in sugar-beet raising, and manufacture into sugar, claim that the soil, climate, etc., of Minnesota is particularly adapted to the cultivation of the sugar beet. Efforts are now being made to introduce the beet-sugar industry in this State. If the venture can be made profitable anywhere, it certainly can be in St. Paul, with its ample facilities for reaching every portion of the agricultural districts of Minnesota and thereby securing the raw material.

OTHER ENTERPRISES THAT WOULD PAY.

There is room in St. Paul for almost every kind of manufacturing industry, but the reader's attention is called particularly to the following, any one of which would be profitable from the very start: Brick yards ; carpet weaving ; broom factories ; fence works ; gloves and mittens : glue works ; hops, malt, etc ; ladies' furnishing goods : notions : lime, plaster, etc. : saddlery goods; tailors' trimmings; vinegar works.

The manufacturer must consider, in conclusion, that there is not only a large market for goods, in all the lines named, at the present time, but that the field of demand is increasing in direct proportion to the wonderful development of the entire Northwest.

MERCHANT's HOTEL, CORNER THIRD AND JACKSON.

Financial Center of the Northwest.

The banks of St. Paul carry the trade of a larger scope of country than those of any American financial center. The natural requirement to this end is the concentration here of comparatively enormous capital. With these facts in mind the reader will learn with less surprise that the resources of the National banks of Minnesota greatly exceed those of Wisconsin, Texas, Colorado, Maryland, Missouri, Kansas, California, Georgia, and twenty other states and territories, while they nearly double those of California, and are twenty-five times greater than the resources of the national banks of Mississippi or Florida. Indeed, the resources of the national banks of St. Paul alone, to say nothing of those of the balance of the State, were, on Jan. 1, 1884, $16,081,786.02, against only $10,680,006 for the entire State of California, $11,864,631 for Kansas, $9,198,935 for Georgia, and largely exceeded the resources of the national banks of any one of nineteen other states and territories. But there is one feature in regard to St Paul's banking development that the reader's attention is called to particularly, and that is the increase of capital during the past year (1883); the official showing presented demonstrating beyond any question St. Paul's supremacy as a financial center, and that it is developing more rapidly in this direction than any city on the continent.

INCREASE IN NATIONAL BANKING CAPITAL.

According to the official report of Hon. J. J. Knox, comptroller of the currency, for the year 1883, Minnesota led every State in the Union, with the single exception of Illinois, in the amount of capital of national banks organized during the year. The amount thus credited to Minnesota is $2,910,000, and of this sum no less than $2,500,000 is represented by the increase in capital of St. Paul national banks. This showing is to the effect, then, that the national banking capital of the city of St. Paul increased more during the year 1883 than did that of the banking capital of any entire State, excepting Illinois. In other words, the national banking capital of St. Paul increased more than 100 per cent during 1883, and the increase was over five times that of all the balance of Minnesota combined. The following table will show that increase, and also the increase in surplus, undivided profits and individual deposits :

YEAR.	Capital st'ck p'd in.	Surplus.	Undivided profits.	Deposits.
1882	$2,200,000	$575,000	$290,368	$8,465,088.64
1883	4,700,000	870,000	384,557	9,473,146.22
Increase	$2,500,000	$295,000	$94,197	$1,008,057.58

INCREASE SINCE 1870.

The following table will show the increase in capital and business of national banks alone in St. Paul since 1870 :

YEAR.	Capital.	Deposits.	Exchange Sold.
1870	$900,000	$1,417,921.00	$16,657,563
1883	4,700,000	9,473,146.22	103,683,070

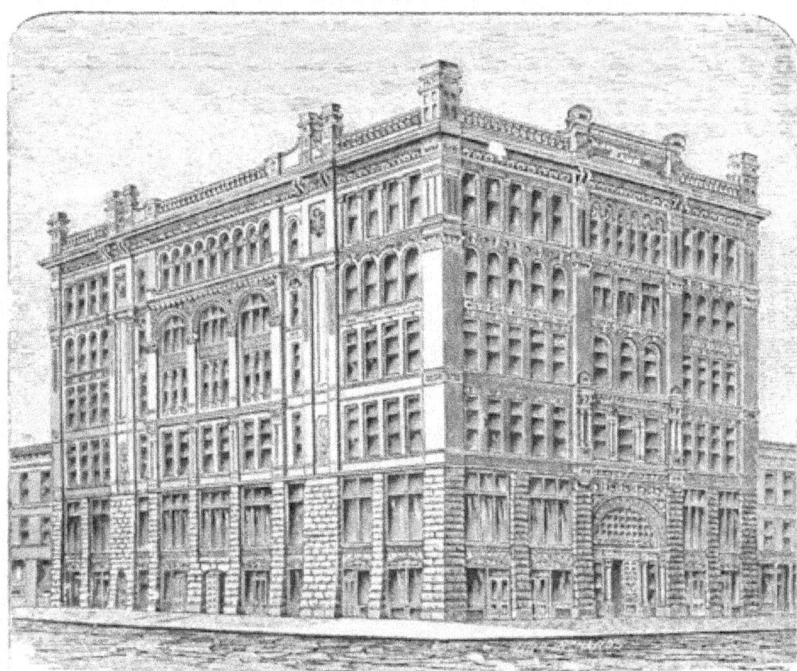

NATIONAL GERMAN-AMERICAN BANK (NOW BUILDING) AT THE CORNER OF FOURTH AND ROBERT STREETS. SIZE, 100x150 FEET, SIX STORIES. WILL COST $200,000 EXCLUSIVE OF GROUND. WILL EQUAL ANY BANK BUILDING IN THE COUNTRY.

OTHER STRIKING STATISTICS.

Iowa and Wisconsin are old States compared with Minnesota, yet the report of the comptroller of the currency shows the following amount of capital, loans and deposits in the national banks of the States named, on October 2, 1883:

STATE.	Capital.	Circulation.	Loans and Discounts.	Individual Deposits.
Minnesota	$9,151,600	$2,126,524	$24,084,505	$17,036,350
Iowa	9,055,000	4,596,303	20,124,327	16,647,922
Wisconsin	4,035,000	2,182,943	13,841,561	14,499,471

In order to make comparisons whereby the reader may be fully able to comprehend the magnitude of St. Paul's banking interests, the same statistics of the national banks of the city are presented, with the balance of Minnesota eliminated:

	Capital and Surplus.	Circulation.	Loans and Discounts.	Individual Deposits.
City of St. Paul	$5,954,361.80	$656,080	$11,504,420.67	$9,473,146.22

From these figures (official) it will be seen that the capital of the national banks of St. Paul is not only larger than the capital of the balance of the Minnesota banks combined, but that it actually exceeds the entire national banking capital of Wisconsin, and is very nearly two-thirds as great as the total national bank capital of Iowa. To form any adequate idea of the importance of St. Paul as a financial center, however, it must be born in mind that the extent to which banks serve the business of any locality is correctly indicated by the volume of loans and discounts and individual deposits, as well (or better) as by the amount of exchange. It is certainly a remarkable showing which St. Paul presents in this regard, for thereby it is seen that the business of all the national banks in Wisconsin combined is less than a fourth greater than those of this city alone, while that of all the national banks of Iowa does not exceed those of St. Paul by over 80 per cent. In making these comparisons the reader must remember that Iowa and Wisconsin are ranked among the most prosperous States in the Union, and far exceed Minnesota in population, yet Minnesota exceeds either of her sister Northwestern States in amount of national bank capital or business.

But individual deposits go a great way in indicating actual amount of business, and it will be noted that the deposits of the St. Paul national banks exceed those of all the balance of national banks in Minnesota combined, by the splendid total of $1,909,942.44.

WHAT THE FIGURES PROVE.

These statistics prove beyond any question that the banks of the city of St. Paul are carrying a vast business that extends far beyond the confines of Minnesota ; that in fact the trade and commerce of the entire Northwest has made St. Paul its financial backer. Now, if this city has attained a position which gives it rank among the chief financial centers of the country—about ninth among the cities of the United States—what are its possibilities when the empire tributary achieves development equal even to that of Wisconsin and Iowa? Even with far less proportionate wealth and population (which at the present rate will be attained by the Northwest within ten years) St. Paul will easily take third place among the money centers, acknowledging only New York and Chicago as superiors. It requires no argument, in these days of money power, to convince the intelligent business man that where ever the financial center of a district is located, there also must concentrate the trade and manufacturing interests of the same region. In other words, St. Paul's acknowledged position as the moneyed power of the Northwest insures beyond any question its future and permanent supremacy in all other lines that contribute to the up-building of a mighty metropolis. Here, and here only, must be located every commercial, industrial and professional pursuit which hopes to prosper by Northwestern patronage.

LOCAL STATISTICS.

In addition to the national banks of St. Paul there are four State banks with a capital of $850,000, and two private banks, each and all doing a large business. One of these State banks exceeds in general resources one of the national banks. A new bank, with a capital of several hundred thousand dollars, has just been organized, but it does not figure in the report of increase of capital, business, etc. The subjoined tables will give the details of increase in business, and will also afford information of the amount of capital, volume of business, etc., of the State banks located in St. Paul, as well as of the national banks.

Financial Condition of the St. Paul Banks at close of Business, Dec. 31, 1883.

RESOURCES.

	Loans and Discounts.	U. S. and other Bonds and Stocks.	Cash.	Due from Banks and U. S. Treasurer.	Real Estate and Fixtures.	Current Expenses & Taxes.	Over-drafts.	Redemption Fund.	Totals.
First National...............	$1,566,523.59	$612,528.21	$629,076.51	$376,972.21			$821.07	$8,655,655	$5,514,612.73
Second National.............	801,276.21	300,000.00	136,141.43	73,638.68	$1,000.00		7,896.01	1,300.00	1,322,493.04
Merchants National...........	2,417,818.16	224,000.95	655,127.03		119,009.35		2,656.22	2,250.00	1,255,506.11
National Ger. Am.............	3,116,279.36	110,302.86	313,365.94	345,186.73	2,000.00		2,656.22		4,034,581.26
Capital Bank.................	283,481.97	129,131.22	79,168.67	82,785.79	4,725.22	$8,358.13	31,462.67		383,291.00
Bank of Minnesota............	1,729,371.78	78,323.80	36,396.00	216,302.79	5,618.87	1,685.08	355.05	2,150,901.64	
Peoples Bank.................	241,752.09	36,617.37	21,690.91	2,463.49	2,578.61	281.23		332,361.51	
Savings Bank of St. Paul.....	158,646.35	15,372.22	24,622.53	18,363.59	2,292.82	285.05	221,623.10	
St. Paul National............	380,613.35	50,000.00	31,918.19	31,619.28	3,402.81	11,351.37	216.85	2,730.00	716,392.85
W. A. Culbertson............. Private Bank.									
A. M. Peabody............... Private Bank.									
	$13,828,550.14	$1,776,552.66	$1,964,497.27	$1,379,481.56	$232,603.02	$19,007.83	$43,412.87	$98,135.65	$19,292,164.80

LIABILITIES.

	Capital Stock Paid in.	Surplus.	Undivided Profits.	Circulation.	Deposits.	Re-discount.	Totals.
First National...............	1,000,000.00	$400,000.00	$53,915.78	$296,000.00	$3,764,616.95		$5,514,612.73
Second National.............	200,000.00	35,000.00	291,696.31	180,000.00	882,826.73		1,322,493.04
Merchants National...........	1,000,000.00	100,000.00	78,252.92	90,000.00	2,772,252.92		4,034,581.26
National Ger. Am.............	2,000,000.00	15,000.00	28,123.69	45,000.00	1,916,457.57		1,955,506.14
Capital Bank.................	100,000.00	25,000.00	29,002.87		358,228.13	$102,504.13	383,291.00
Bank of Minnesota............	100,000.00	20,000.00	27,203.97		1,341,265.54		2,150,901.64
Peoples Bank.................	20,000.00	5,000.00	6,501.36		271,859.58		332,361.51
Savings Bank of St. Paul.....	100,000.00	5,000.00	11,704.63		169,596.45		221,623.10
St. Paul National............	100,000.00	100,000.00	24,601.10	45,000.00	146,991.75		716,392.85
W. A. Culbertson............. Private Bank.							
A. M. Peabody............... Private Bank.							
	5,550,000.00	$800,000.00	$430,132.85	$636,000.00	$11,552,617.52	$102,504.13	$19,292,164.80

RESOURCES — RECAPITULATION BY TOTALS.

	1882.	1883.	Increase.	Decrease.
Loans and discounts	$10,870,091.15	$13,838,559.14	$2,968,467.99	
United States and other bonds	1,634,512.49	1,776,352.66	142,040.17	
Cash	1,536,395.01	1,964,407.27	428,012.26	
Due from banks and U. S. treasurer	1,142,477.56	1,379,484.56	237,007.00	
Real estate and fixtures	109,416.70	252,605.02	143,188.32	
Current expenses and taxes	18,727.61	19,007.13	279.52	
Overdrafts	40,406.92	43,412.87	3,005.95	
Redemption fund	49,675.10	18,135.65		$31,539.45
Totals	$15,401,702.54	$19,292,164.30	$3,922,001.21	$31,539.45

LIABILITIES — RECAPITULATION BY TOTALS.

	1882.	1883.	Increase.	Decrease.
Capital stock	$3,250,000.00	$5,550,000.00	$2,300,000.00	
Surplus	745,000.00	930,000.00	185,000.00	
Profits	382,433.78	450,132.85	67,699.07	
Circulation	554,780.00	656,080.00	101,300.00	
Deposits	10,395,724.70	11,553,617.32	1,157,892.62	
Re-discounts	73,764.06	152,334.13	78,570.07	
Totals	$15,401,702.54	$19,292,164.30	$3,890,461.76	

TOTAL BANKING CAPITAL OF ST. PAUL.

By the tables above presented it will be seen that the total banking capital of St. Paul, state and national, is the magnificent sum of $6,930,132.85, including surplus and undivided profits, and that the total resources are $19,292,164.30.

BANK BUILDINGS.

The prosperity of St. Paul banking institutions is somewhat indicated by the number of splendid new bank edifices now building. The First National is just completing a structure at the corner of Fourth and Jackson streets which has cost upward of $100,000. The National German-American is building a bank structure at the corner of Fourth and Robert streets which will be 100 x 150 feet, six stories, and will cost over $200,000. The Merchants' National and Second National are already located in fine buildings. The Bank of Minnesota has just decided to build a $100,000 building, and the Capital Bank has plans perfected for a very fine new structure.

ROOM FOR NEW BANKS.

The figures given, indicating as they do the remarkable increase in banking business in St. Paul, are the best possible argument that additional capital may be used to advantage in banking in this city. The capitalist who comprehends the certainty of northwestern development need not be told that the present banking facilities of St. Paul will be unable to meet the trade requirements of a very few years hence. In this line St. Paul offers inducements that the trained banker cannot fail to appreciate.

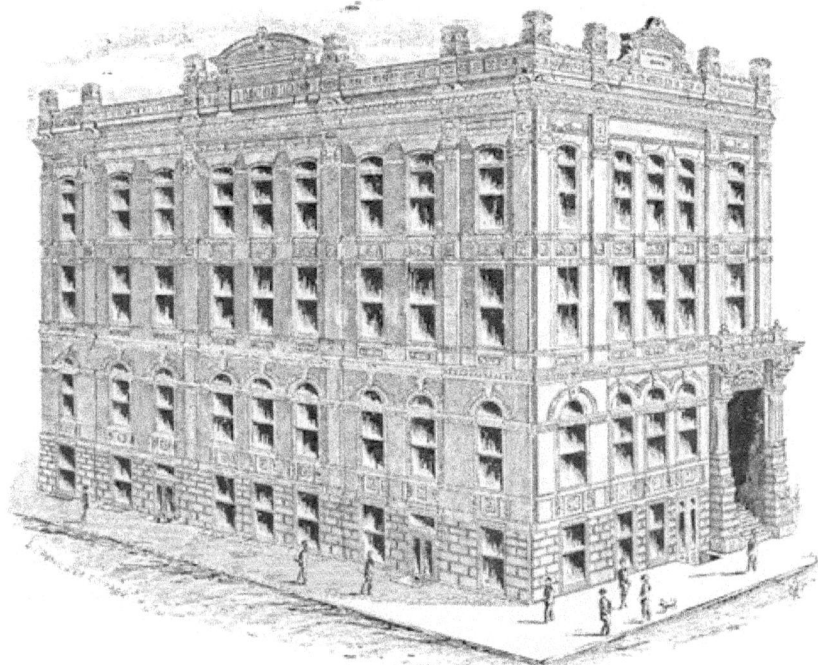

THE ABOVE REPRESENTATION IS OF THE NEW BUILDING OF THE FIRST NATIONAL BANK, CORNER OF FOURTH AND JACKSON. THE EDIFICE IS 50x100 FEET, FOUR STORIES, AND COST, EXCLUSIVE OF GROUND, OVER $100,000.

Social Advantages.

St. Paul may well claim special social advantages. It is the capital of the State, and is therefore the temporary residence, at least, of the State officials and their families. It is the seat of justice of the commonwealth, and, therefore, the concentrating point of the talent and culture of the bar of the State. Here are located the federal officers who are intrusted with the business of the general government. Near at hand, at Fort Snelling, are established the military headquarters of one of the great departments of the army, affording in its officers and their families a select and cultured society. St. Paul is also the home of very many wealthy and retired gentlemen who have sought, with their families, the health-giving climate of this region, and find here educational and living advantages which induce permanent location. Further than the advantages thus mentioned, the early settlement of the town was by a class of persons connected with the army or representing wealth enough to engage in the fur trade: establishing a nucleus of wealth and consequent social requirements that even to this day are apparent in the leading circles. The fact that St. Paul has always been the capital of Minnesota, of course attracted from the first whatever there was of culture and education in the immigration to the the new State. The general result has been the formation and continuence of as refined social circles as are to be met with in any city of the Union.

St. Paul's Railway System.

St. Paul is not only the railway center of the Northwest, but it is also one of the chief radiating points of the grand system of American roads. Here are located the headquarters and principal terminus of the Northern Pacific, the shortest and most important route from the Mississippi valley to the Pacific coast. From this city the St. Paul, Minneapolis & Manitoba lines strike out to make tributary the great valley of the Red River of the North and the territory of Manitoba; and here are established the headquarters of the company, its shops and all its terminal facilities. In St. Paul also are the headquarters, sh ps, etc., of the Omaha line, which gives a through route to San Francisco considerably shorter than any from Chicago. Here are the shops, general offices and all terminal grounds of the St. Paul and Duluth road. Division offices of the Chicago, Milwaukee & St. Paul are maintained here, while the same is true of the various other lines out of this city. Statistics given below will indicate somewhat the present importance of St. Paul as a railway center, but they cannot form anything more than a slight basis upon which to establish clear comprehension of the mighty future of the city as a railway metropolis when the now undeveloped empire West and Northwest shall be afforded traffic facilities equal to those of older sections of the Union. The country tributary to St. Paul is richer and far vaster than that from which Chicago has derived its greatness, and the day is not distant when this city will become an equally important railway center with Chicago.

A brief official statement, with reference to railway constructio n in this country in 1882, conveys so clear a hint in regard to St. Paul's importance as a railway center that it may properly introduce the statistical information to be presented in this chapter:

"The number of miles of railway constructed in the United States during 1882 was 11,000, of which 2,400 miles, or nearly one-fourth of the grand total, is credited to the system centering in St. Paul."

At the present time there are five great railway systems in the United States, and five recognized railway centers. The order of rank in importance, accepted in commercial, as well as railway circles, gives Chicago and the Central system, first place; New York and the Eastern system, second place; St. Paul and the Northwestern system, third place; St. Louis and the Southwestern system, fourth place; and Cincinnati and the Southern system, fifth place. The position attained by St. Paul is practically the result of less than ten years development, for in 1873, the Northern Pacific — upon the building of which the Northwestern system depended — was as much a failure as it now is a success. The map of "St. Paul Railways and their Connections," presented as an appropriate frontispiece to this pamphlet, will indicate somewhat the maze of iron tracks radiating to every point of the compass from this center, but it can convey no idea of the boundless wealth of territory, trade and population made tributary by them to St. Paul. Neither will mere statistics of miles of railways operated by this system suffice to give the reader a clear understanding of the magnitude of interests concentrated thereby in this city. To arrive at anything like an accurate appreciation of the general situation, the reader must supplement this chapter by those referring to the territory tributary to St. Paul, the location of the city, trade statistics, etc.

MAIN LINES CENTERING IN ST. PAUL.

There are now ten great corporations running regular trains into St. Paul over their own and other lines, while three of them have two or more entirely distinct

General Offices of the Northern Pacific R. R.

NORTHERN PACIFIC HEADQUARTERS. COST, EXCLUSIVE OF GROUNDS, $165,000.

and different routes to and from this point.   The St. Paul Union Depot time table
issued Jan. 1, 1884, gives the total number of passenger trains in and out of the
depot daily (all but four of them between the hours of 6 A. M. and 9 P. M.) as one
hundred and sixty-four, tabulated as follows:

Corporation.	Number of Passenger Trains.
Chicago, Milwaukee & St. Paul	50
St. Paul, Minneapolis & Manitoba	50
Chicago, St. Paul, Minneapolis & Omaha	38
St. Paul & Duluth	14
Minneapolis & St. Louis	8
Northern Pacific	4
Total	164

The recent annual report of Gen. Baker, railroad commissioner of Minnesota,
gives the following statistics relative to mileage, equipment and number of
employees of the roads centering at St. Paul:

GENERAL EQUIPMENT.

NAME OF ROAD.	No. of Employees.	No. of Locomotiv's	No. of Cars.	Miles of road Operated.
Chicago, Milwaukee & St. Paul	21,268	639	19,063	4,514
St. Paul, Minneapolis & Manitoba	7,300	291	5,068	1,329
Chicago & Northwestern	15,970	580	18,907	3,584
Northern Pacific	8,578	239	6,796	1,701
St. Paul & Duluth	1,251	34	1,023	208
Minneapolis & St. Louis	1,687	69	2,150	420
Chicago, St. Paul, Minneapolis & Omaha	5,866	181	5,322	1,142
Burlington, Cedar Rapids & Northern	2,233	77	3,669	713
Totals	64,153	212	61,872	13,611

Of the total number of 64,153 employees, over 14,000 are employed within
the limits of the State of Minnesota; a very large proportion in St. Paul.
Of the Chicago, St. Paul, Minneapolis & Omaha trains, four of them are
properly Chicago & Northwestern through trains, two are distinctively St. Paul &
Sioux City, and two are utilized by the Wisconsin Central — now building its own
line into this city.   Of the Minneapolis & St. Louis passenger trains two are
properly Burlington, and two Rock Island — thus affording passenger facilities by
ten trunk lines that, by their connections, make available every mile of railway
in America.   So complete is the time table arrangement of the roads that scarcely
an hour of the day passes without witnessing the arrival or departure of great
through trains to Chicago, St. Louis, Omaha, Winnipeg, Lake Superior points and
the Pacific coast.

THE ROADS AND THEIR CONNECTIONS.

By right of direct importance to the future development of St. Paul, the Northern Pacific railway is entitled to first consideration in these pages.   Here are all of
the general offices of the great national highway, grouped together in one of the
most costly and imposing railway office buildings in America.   The edifice is four
stories high, built of finest pressed brick, with Perth Amboy terra cotta trimmings,
fronts on Broadway and directly west on Fourth street, cost $165,000, is absolutely
fire proof, and is a model of convenience for railway office use.   St. Paul being officially proclaimed the principal terminus of the road it naturally followed that all
of the shops, terminal grounds, etc., would be located here.   To that end the company wisely determined to secure acreage enough in St. Paul to ever avoid the
possibility of being cramped for terminal room, and therefore purchased nearly

Union Depot.

four hundred acres of land, one-half of which extends from the present business center of the city to extensive grounds in the northern portion of town, and two hundred acres adjoining the city limits on the west. The latter area is intended for stock yards, elevators, etc., while the former will be devoted to shops, depots, warehouses, yard room and general terminal purposes. Leaving St. Paul, the tracks of the Northern Pacific extend in a northwesterly direction to Brainerd, Minn., whence a spur runs east to Duluth on Lake Superior; from Brainerd the line runs but little north of west to Moorhead, where the Red river of the north is crossed and a direct west course is taken over the plains of Dakota. Entering Montana just beyond the crossing of the Little Missouri, the route is south of west up the valley of the Yellowstone to Livingston, when it runs northwesterly until Northern Idaho is crossed, where it turns southerly again to Ainsworth in Washington, northerly to Tacoma and south to Portland, Oregon; thereby affording the shortest and best route from the valley of the Mississippi to the Pacific ocean, and opening up one of the most fertile and prolific regions of the earth. This is the main line of the Northern Pacific, with 1,701 miles operated, but it does not indicate the complete system of the company which, when feeders now under construction or contemplated are built, will increase the total mileage to 4,000.

ST. PAUL, MINNEAPOLIS & MANITOBA.

This system, with 1,329 miles of road operated, and a number of feeders under construction, is also distinctly a St. Paul road, having its headquarters in a fine block, built expressly for the purpose, on Fourth street, and all its shops and terminal facilities here. The president and principal officers of the company are long time residents of this city. To the St. Paul, Minneapolis & Manitoba company is the credit due of opening up the west and northwest portion of Minnesota and the Red river valley, and making tributary Winnipeg and the British provinces. The corporation has two lines penetrating the region designated, and it is the great outlet of a vast agricultural region of almost limitless capacity, which is dependent wholly upon St. Paul as a trade center.

LAKE SUPERIOR ROUTES.

St. Paul has two direct routes to Lake Superior points, and others are now building. The most important of these is the St. Paul & Duluth road, which, although operating over 200 miles of road, has a direct line of 155 miles in length, uniting St. Paul and Duluth. This route gives St. Paul cheap and easy access to lake navigation, with all of the advantages it may possess. Its headquarters and general offices are located on Fourth street, St. Paul, and while it now has extensive shops, it is preparing to build new ones of larger capacity.

The Chicago, St. Paul, Minneapolis & Omaha also operates lines to Lake Superior, by one reaching Superior City, and the other Bayfield and Washburne.

The completion of the Wisconsin Central will add still further to St. Paul's facilities for controlling the business of the Lake Superior region.

SOUTHEASTERN AND SOUTHERN LINES.

It is fairly a network of iron tracks that center in St. Paul from the east-southeast and south. First in importance is the Chicago, Milwaukee & St. Paul with its two great routes—widely separated—leading from St. Paul to all points east and south. By its river line all the Mississippi river towns, from La Crosse north, are placed in close connection with this city, while by the Prairie du Chien system the principal cities of central and southern Minnesota are equally favored.

The Chicago, St. Paul, Minneapolis and Omaha, together with the Chicago & Northwestern (comprised in one system) affords equal facilities with the Chicago, Milwaukee & St. Paul for reaching Chicago, and at the same time makes tributary to this city a large portion of Wisconsin. The permanent headquarters of the Chicago, St. Paul, Minneapolis & Omaha are located here in a fine general office build-

St. Paul, Minneapolis & Manitoba.
General Office.

St. Paul, Minneapolis & Omaha
General Office.

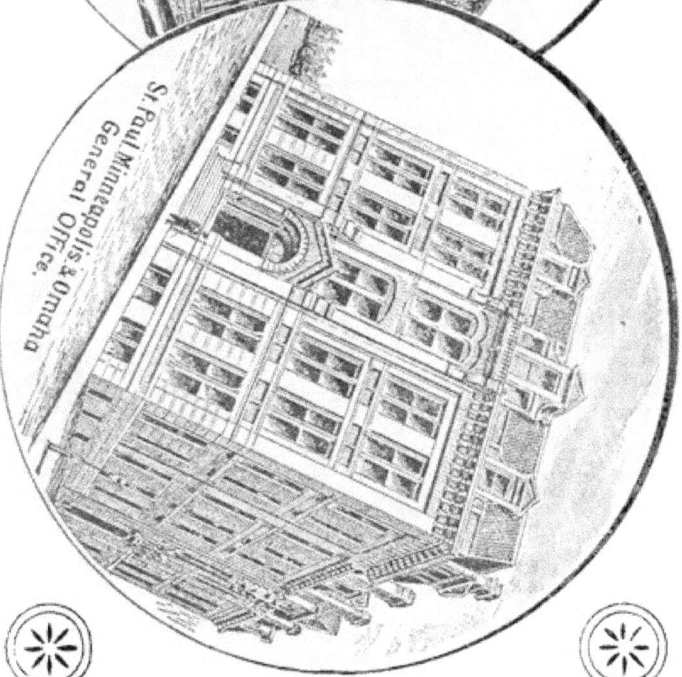

Among the finest railway office buildings in the West. Were built expressly for the use of the respective companies.

ing. and its shops at this point are extensive. It is doing. and has done, more to make Northern Wisconsin tributary to St. Paul — to say nothing of the southwest — than any other corporation.

By these lines and the Minneapolis & St. Louis and its connections. St. Louis. New Orleans and all Southern points are reached by several different daily trains on nearly air lines between St. Paul and the large Southern cities of the Mississippi valley.

WEST AND SOUTHWESTERN ROADS.

The due west and southwest are made accessible from St. Paul by the Chicago & Northwestern, which has penetrated as far west as Pierre on the Missouri river — half way across Dakota and just a trifle south of west of this city ; the Chicago, Milwaukee & St. Paul. which has also reached the Missouri at Chamberlain. and has still another line running due west from St. Paul to Aberdeen and other points in Dakota ; the Chicago, St. Paul, Minneapolis & Omaha running to Sioux City in Iowa, and thence to Omaha, and the direct route to San Francisco, opening up the entire southwestern part of Minnesota, Northwestern Iowa and Eastern Nebraska ; the Minneapolis & St. Louis running due south and combining with the Rock Island and Burlington, Cedar Rapids & Northern.

LOCAL IMPROVEMENTS BY THE ROADS.

The money expended by the St. Paul roads in 1882, in local improvements. aggregated $830,000. This sum was nearly doubled in 1883. The record for the two years is as follows :

Road.	1882.	1883.
Northern Pacific	$ 250,000	$ 750,000
St. Paul, Minneapolis & Manitoba	484,500	650,000
Chicago, Milwaukee & St. Paul		90,000
Chicago, St. Paul, Minneapolis & Omaha	71,000	55,000
St. Paul & Duluth	12,500	3,000
Union Depot	12,500	
Totals	$830,000	$1,548,000

NEW MILEAGE AND ITS COST.

The total new mileage added to the St. Paul system in 1883 was 1.319. as follows :

Road.	Miles of Track laid.	Total cost.
Northern Pacific	753	$15,100,000
St. Paul, Minneapolis & Manitoba	86	3,686,500
Chicago, Milwaukee & St. Paul	170	2,710,000
Chicago & Northwestern	141	2,500,000
Chicago, St. Paul, Minneapolis & Omaha	145	1,430,000
St. Paul & Duluth	16	240,000
Minneapolis & St. Louis	3	170,000
Totals	1,319	$25,836,500

The total number of miles of road added to the St. Paul system during the past three years is 7,200.

NEW ROADS NOW BUILDING AND PROJECTED.

Complete as the St. Paul railway system seems, it is yet in its infancy. Proof of this is afforded in the present rush of new lines for this center. All through the cold weather of the present winter surveying parties, representing different railway corporations. have been running and locating lines into St. Paul.

CHICAGO, BURLINGTON & QUINCY.

First is the Chicago, Burlington & Quincy, which, under the charter of the Chicago, St. Paul & St. Louis, will complete its road to this city sometime during

the coming summer.   The route will be directly up the valley of the Mississippi.
and will give an entirely new, direct and independent line to Chicago and St.
Louis and the great general systems of this important corporation.   St. Paul will
be made its northern terminus, and it will add largely to the railway resources
now enjoyed.   Construction work is in progress.

WISCONSIN CENTRAL.

Next is the Wisconsin Central, which has its survey from Chippewa Falls, Wis.,
to St. Paul completed (directly from the East), and expects to finish the road to
this point before December.   This line will give a new and direct road to the very
heart of the Wisconsin pineries, will afford a new route to Milwaukee and a new
line to Lake Superior.   St. Paul will be its western terminus and will probably
secure its most important shops.   Construction work is to begin immediately.

MINNESOTA & NORTHWESTERN.

A very important new line, on which construction work will begin as soon as
spring weather will permit, is the Minnesota & Northwestern, which is to run
directly south from St. Paul to Mona, Iowa, to which point it will connect with the
Illinois Central, and give a new and very direct route from St. Paul to the Gulf of
Mexico.   The name "Minnesota & Northwestern" is supposed to be the style
under which the Illinois Central prefers to work in reaching this city.   The line is
located, and work will begin this spring at the St. Paul end.   St. Paul will be the
principal terminus aside from Chicago.   The local improvements required here
will be extensive

ST. PAUL EASTERN GRAND TRUNK.

This road is now building from Oconto, Wis., on the shores of Green Bay,
directly west to St. Paul.   It will be completed to Wausau, Wis., about 170
miles, this season, when it will have access to this city over other lines.   It will
be completed to this point as soon as practicable, and St. Paul will then become
its headquarters and principal terminus.   It will not only afford the nearest route
to a Lake Michigan port (300 miles due east), but will tap every pinery in Wisconsin, and will give a short line to the iron and copper mines of Michigan.

SAULT STE. MARIE.

The Sault Ste. Marie road, which is to run from Minneapolis and St. Paul a
trifle north of east across Wisconsin and northern Michigan to the Sault Ste. Marie,
will also tap all of the pineries of Wisconsin and mines of Michigan, and will be
a very important outlet to the East for Northwestern products.   Work upon it will
begin as soon as spring opens, and will be pushed with all possible vigor.   It is
said to be the purpose of this corporation to complete a line clear to the Atlantic
seaboard.

The above roads are certain to be built to or from St. Paul this season, with
the single exception of the St. Paul Eastern Grand Trunk.   Of roads that are
known to be seeking direct entrance into St. Paul over their own tracks (and
which are pretty sure to be built within a few years), may be mentioned the Green
Bay, Winona & St. Paul; Davenport & St. Paul (old line revived); Rock Island;
a line to Mille Lacs, tapping Minnesota pineries (recently organized), and the
Chicago & Superior, whenever that project is pushed.

Of roads now building in Minnesota one of the most important is the Duluth
& Iron Range which is being pushed rapidly from Lake Superior to the great iron
mines at Vermillion Lake.

So far as railway facilities in Minnesota are concerned — making the vast
resources of the State more or less directly tributary to St. Paul — a complete summary is given in this terse sentence in the report of Railroad Commissioner Baker :
"Of the seventy-nine counties in the state, seventy-three are now supplied with
reasonable railway facilities."

The statistics above given may prove somewhat bewildering to readers who are not familiar from personal observation with the gigantic railway development of the Northwest during the past few years, yet they are taken in all instances from official sources ; and they are as much an indication of what the future is to vouch-safe to St. Paul in way of commercial greatness, as they are proof of what has already been accomplished.

Territory Tributary to St. Paul.

The region directly, and in large part exclusively, tributary to St. Paul as a trade center by reason of its railway system, embraces the northern half of Wisconsin, Minnesota, a portion of Northern Iowa, Dakota, Wyoming, Montana, Idaho, Oregon, Washington Territory, and Manitoba, and the northwestern part of the Dominion of Canada.   The area of this district, exclusive of that of the Dominion of Canada, is over one-fourth of the entire area of the United States, and comprises the best agricultural, timber, grazing and mineral lands of the continent.   Statistics of square miles are as follows :

Territory.	No. Square Miles.	
Area of the United States		2,936,166
Tributary to St. Paul.		
North half of Wisconsin	27,000	
Minnesota	81,259	
Portion of Iowa	15,000	
Dakota	150,932	
Wyoming	97,883	
Montana	145,776	
Idaho	86,300	
Oregon	95,274	
Washington	69,994	
Total area within United States	769,418	2,936,166
Manitoba	154,411	
Total area tributary to St. Paul	923,829	

Including the British province of Manitoba, the area directly tributary to St. Paul is equal in extent to nearly one-third of the United States.   It is only by comparison with other, and older and better known countries, that the real magnitude of this domain can be appreciated by the general reader.   For instance, this northwestern empire might include within its boundaries all of Germany, France, Norway, Sweden, Holland and Denmark, and still have nearly ground enough left to make a second German empire.   In other words, the total number of square miles in Germany, France, Norway, Sweden, Holland and Denmark is 741,602, while the area of the district tributary to St. Paul is 923,829 square miles. Nor is mere extent of territory all that is to be considered, for there is more waste land (that it is not possible to utilize for any purpose) in the combined European countries named than there is in the American domain under consideration.   Of the two portions of continents compared, the American is richer in general resources, and presents a better average of climatic conditions.

This vast region of immeasurable natural wealth is not only geographically tributary to St. Paul, but by railways already constructed it is united more closely to this city than to any other metropolis.   Not only that, but all present and prospective railway building throughout the Territory under discussion is projected on the basis of making St. Paul the principal terminus or depot.   To arrive at

the exact relations of this domain with St. Paul, and the present and prospective
importance to this city of that relationship, it becomes necessary to refer briefly
to the various resources and development of the States and Territories specified,
and to the railroad system which makes them tributary to this commercial center:

NORTH HALF OF WISCONSIN.

An hour's ride by rail on any one of three different railway lines will place
the traveler in Wisconsin. Geographically, St. Paul is situate but a little north
of the central east and west line of Wisconsin, and is, therefore, a much nearer
market for the northern half of the State than is Milwaukee. It is only within a
few years that the immense natural resources of Northern Wisconsin began to be
appreciated, and hence its development was slow in comparison with that of the
southern portion of the State. Within the last decade, however, Northern Wisconsin has stepped from the position of an almost unknown wilderness to an
importance quite overshadowing the southern half of the commonwealth. All of
the vast timber and mineral wealth of Wisconsin lies north of the center of the
State, and is, therefore, tributary to St. Paul. These vast pineries now cut upward
of two billion feet of lumber annually; and while lack of railway facilities, up to
a few years ago, prevented this enormous product from seeking Northwestern prairies via St. Paul, the present lines now operated have turned a large portion to this
market; and railways now building will, within two years at most, give St. Paul
practical control over the bulk of the immense lumber product of Wisconsin. Up
to within a very few years, Chicago and St. Louis absolutely controlled the timber
cut of Wisconsin, but now, even with present railway facilities, St. Paul is the
largest market-factor in the calculations of the lumbermen of that State. At
present lumber from a portion of the Wisconsin pineries may reach St. Paul by
various lines of the Chicago, St. Paul, Minneapolis & Omaha road and the Chicago, Milwaukee & St. Paul; and through connections may find this market from
a number of interior lines. But the early completion of the Wisconsin Central to
this point (now assured) will fairly lift the flood gates of Wisconsin's greatest
product and pour its tide directly into this city. The building of the St. Paul
Eastern Grand Trunk railway—from Oconto, Wis., to St. Paul—will connect
every pinery of the sister State immediately with this market; and the projected
road to the Sault Ste. Marie (certain to be built within two years) will also become
one of the great outlets for Wisconsin lumber. It is not too much to say that
within two years St. Paul will easily control the entire lumber product of Wisconsin.

Wisconsin is scarcely less oppulent in iron ores than she is in timber growth;
and as the mines of the State all lie in the northern portion, the same railway
facilities that control the lumber cut will also make the iron mines tributary.

The system of railways now developing will also place St. Paul in direct connection with the iron mines of the Peninsula of Michigan and the copper mines of
Lake Superior. The day is not far distant, indeed, when both the iron and copper
products of Michigan will find their nearest market in St. Paul.

The rapid development of Northern Wisconsin has also placed a population of
about 300,000 in quick communication and intercourse with St. Paul. The means
of communication are perfecting daily, while even now more than one-half of this
population consider St. Paul their natural metropolis.

MINNESOTA.

Minnesota, of which St. Paul is the capital, occupies very nearly the geographical center of the continent of North America. The general physical characteristic is that of an undulating plain. It is the highest land between the Gulf of
Mexico and Hudson Bay (average elevation above the sea, 1,000 feet) and forms
the watershed of the three great river systems of the country. The general development of Minnesota is something wonderful, the population of the State having
increased from 172,023 in 1860 to 780,806 in 1880 and 1,000,000 (estimated) in

1883. Of the 53,353,600 acres comprising the area of the State, 2,700,000 acres are in beautiful lakes varying in size from one mile to thirty in diameter, and numbering no less than 7,000 distinct bodies of spring-like water. It is estimated that of this total acreage over 15,000,000 acres are richest prairie, nearly all of which has been taken in small parcels by actual settlers. Minnesota, indeed, ranks among the very first wheat producing States of the Union, 40,000,000 bushels being an average yearly product ; while hay, oats, corn, potatoes, barley, rye and buckwheat follow in importance in the order named.   Dairy products follow close upon the agricultural in value, while horse, cattle, sheep and hog products are yearly becoming of more and more importance. All in all, Minnesota is one of the foremost agricultural States of the Union.   Its natural wealth, however, is not confined to its fertile acres, for it is one of the great lumber producing regions of the country and has standing to-day as much pine timber as either Wisconsin or Michigan.   In addition to the great bodies of pine, there are vast forests of choicest hardwoods which will ere long be a source of profit. Of late Minnesota is acquiring importance in an entirely unlookedfor direction, that of mineral wealth.   It is now certain that the largest and most valuable iron ore deposit yet discovered in America is wholly within the limits of the State. Reference is made to the Vermillion iron mines, two hundred miles north of St. Paul, to which the Duluth & Iron Range railway is now building.   These ores are inexhaustible, are the hard or specular hematite, and are said by experts to be the best Bessemer ores yet found in this country.   The silver and copper mines of Minnesota are beginning to attract attention.   From the Pigeon river, on the north shore of Lake Superior, to Duluth at the head of the great lake, there have been numerous discoveries of both copper and silver mines, some of which are now being worked and promise to become important and profitable.   An important resource of Minnesota lies in the splendid quarries of slate, granite, sandstone and limestone that abound in the State.   On the St. Louis river the slate quarries are large and of good quality. From the same region comes the Fond du Lac stone — purple sandstone — which is acknowledged to be one of the most beautiful building stones ever utilized.   Minnesota granite is already famous for its beauty and excellence, and is found in inexhaustible quarries of various colors, composition, etc., at Sauk Rapids.   From Kasota is brought an orange-tinted sandstone of great durability.   At St. Paul are vast quarries of limestone.

Minnesota combines, then, three great material resource of wealth and population, agriculture, lumbering and mining. The capablities of the State are practically unlimited, as compared with sterile New England or restricted Middle States.   It has developed railway facilities more rapidly than any Northwestern State, now having no less than six great trunk lines extending across the State from east to west, and southwest and northwest ; while it has two connections with Lake Superior by rail ; practically two with Winnipeg and the Dominion of Canada ; and the southern portion is fairly a net-work of iron tracks.   There are now operated within the limits of Minnesota 3,578.33-100 miles of railway, costing, with equipment, $159 071,150.44.   Of this railway system St. Paul is the acknowledged center.

In addition to Minnesota's railways, she has transportation facilities by way of Lake Superior, and five navigable rivers with a water line of over 1,500 miles.

In way of possibilities of development, Minnesota may easily rival any of the Eastern or Middle States.   The area of territory is greater than that of New York, New Jersey, Delaware, Massachusetts, Connecticut and Vermont combined, and is more than double that of Ohio.

DAKOTA.

Dakota is the largest territory in the Union and is exceeded in area by only two States, Texas and California.   It would make one hundred and nineteen states the size of Rhode Island ; and thirty-two the size of Connecticut.   The number of acres is 96,596,480.   This Territory, together with Minnesota, is the largest and best hard wheat producing country in the world. Of all this vast region of 96,596,480 acres, by far the larger half is the very best agricultural or grazing land. In Northeastern and Southeastern Dakota the soil is a calcareous loam of great fertility, averaging several feet in depth. The western portion is particularly adapted to cattle raising. The future possibilities of the agricultural and grazing districts are incalculable. Dakota is also rich in minerals; coal is abundant on the Missouri river, iron, lead, salt and petroleum have been discovered, while the famous Black Hills district is one of the most productive gold regions in America. About 1,500 miles of railway now t averse the Territory, by means of which direct communication is had with St. Paul. No section of the United States is developing more rapidly in population than Dakota ; and it is the site of a future empire of boundless wealth directly tributary to this city.

MONTANA.

Montana comprises 92,000,000 acres of land — but little less than Dakota — of which 10,000,000 are classed as agricultural, 38,000,000 grazing; 12,000,000 pine timber, and 26,000,000 mineral and mountainous. Montana is now famous for its grazing advantages, and recent estimates place the present stock of cattle, sheep and horses at not less than 2,000,000 head. Montana has suddenly become, in fact, the rival of Texas and the Southwest as the cattle, sheep and wool producing section of the United States. The climate of Montana is much warmer than that of Eastern States in the same latitude, and is very dry, the rainfall rarely exceeding twelve inches per annum. While the snowfall is heavy in the mountains it is light in the valleys, and hence is favorable to stock-raising and agricultural pursuits. It is one of the richest mining countries in the world, containing within its borders gold, silver, copper, lead, coal and other valuable minerals. Mining operations were begun in 1861, and it is estimated that nearly $200,000,000 worth of gold and silver has been obtained since that time. The Northern Pacific railway traverses Montana from east to west, thus affording an outlet to St. Paul of the vast and long-imprisoned wealth of this great Territory. With an area more than three times as great as that of New York, what may be expected of its possibilities of development? It already acknowledges St. Paul as its commercial metropolis.

WYOMING.

The area of Wyoming is 62,645,120 acres. It is asserted by those most familiar with the Territory that fully one-half of its entire area consists of grazing lands of the richest character. Its mountains are rich in minerals. Its chief attraction at present is the famous Yellowstone Park, reached by a branch road of the Northern Pacific from Livingston. Its herds nearly equal those of Montana.

IDAHO.

The Northern Pacific crosses the northern portion of Idaho. The area in acres is 55,228,160. The valleys are fertile, but it is in its mines that the wealth of this Territory exists. Just now the gold discoveries in the Cœur d'Alene range are attracting special attention. Idaho is remarkable for its majestic scenery, and will become a favorite resort for tourists. In mineral wealth it is probably unsurpassed by any of the western region.

WASHINGTON AND OREGON.

Washington Territory has an area of 45,000,000 acres, and Oregon 64,000,000. Washington and Oregon are usually styled the "Pacific Northwest," and are considered richer in general and natural resources than almost any like area in the United States. While this region produces astonishing crops of wheat, oats, barley, rye, hops, etc., its chief natural wealth is timber, of which it may be said there is absolutely an inexhaustible supply. It is claimed, indeed, that the finest body of timber in the world is embraced between the Columbia river and British Columbia, and the Pacific and the Cascades. The fisheries and mines are also of importance.

Imperfect as is this summary of the leading features of the vast Northwest, the reader will readily discover that it is a region of limitless possibilities of wealth and population. Unlike the region traversed by the Union Pacific, almost every mile through which the Northern Pacific runs is valuable for either agricultural, grazing, mining or lumbering purposes. This condition of things means that while it will ever be impossible to sustain a large population along the Central route to the Pacific, the territory of the Northern line will become in time densely peopled ; and St. Paul will continue to be the metropolis of this mighty region.

MANITOBA.

The British province of Manitoba joins Minnesota and a portion of Dakota on the north, and is nearly equal in area to Dakota, comprising 154,411 square miles. Its chief city, Winnipeg, is connected by rail with St. Paul — the only rail route south — so that the province is directly tributary to this city. Manitoba is almost one vast prairie, and will, therefore, in time become a great wheat producing district. The soil is of remarkable fertility, and rye, barley and potatoes are easily raised, although wheat must ever be its chief production. Its mineral resources are also attracting attention, and marked indications of rich mines of precious metals have been found, the development of which has already begun. The country is settling rapidly and promises a notable advancement in general growth of wealth and population. Its entire trade is in or through St. Paul the greater portion of the year.

Educational Facilities.

It is fortunate for St. Paul that the leading and governing minds in the public policy of the city have been in favor of unstinted means and measures for increasing and perfecting educational facilities, both public and private. The result is unsurpassed graded and high school advantages, and academic and collegiate opportunities. Persons who move from Eastern cities to become residents of St. Paul are invariably surprised to find here finer, larger and more suitable school buildings than they have been accustomed to in their cultured homes in the older cities. They look with surprise upon a high school edifice which has cost $135,-000; they note with gratification buildings for graded school purposes that are valued at $60,000. When they discover that there are no less than seventeen of these costly public schools already accommodating the children of the city, and five new ones to be constructed during 1884, their possible anticipation of having brought their children into a country cross-roads district to be educated is at once dispelled. Indeed, they soon learn that St. Paul, with the liberality, energy and common sense of new Western towns, far surpasses the conservative expenditures of Eastern cities in the direction of general education. Wealth is acquired easily and quickly in a locality where development is so rapid as it is in the Northwest, and things which would be considered an extravagance in the older sections of country are here deemed of common necessity. This rule applies to an admirable purpose when it serves educational advancement, and nowhere is its application more evident than in St. Paul. The aim, in fact, has been to develop here both public and private scholastic facilities equal to any to be found in the country. It has been a special endeavor on the part of prominent and controlling citizens, without regard to religious or political considerations, to make the schools of St. Paul worthy the evident future of the city; and the success attained is a matter of just pride.

HIGH SCHOOL BUILDING. COST $125,000.

THE PUBLIC SCHOOLS.

Up to the present time St. Paul has expended over half a million dollars in substantial brick or stone public school buildings and sites, and expects to expend $100,000 the present season in the erection of five new structures. The present buildings and their cost are listed as follows:

SCHOOL.	VALUE.	SCHOOL.	VALUE.
High School	$135,000	Rice	$5,000
Franklin	60,000	River	9,000
Humboldt	9,000	Webster	19,000
Jefferson	45,000	Washington	22,000
Jackson	13,000	Harrison	4,500
Lincoln	36,000	Garfield	18,000
Madison	50,000	Adams	13,000
Monroe	15,000		
Neill	15,000	Total	$503,500
Van Buren	35,000		

The structures to be erected this year will be new Humboldt, Neill and Rice schools, a costly addition to the Adams, and a fine building in East St. Paul.

The illustration of the high school presented herein does not do the structure justice, as a square front view shows the fine architecture to best advantage. The building is one of the finest of its class anywhere, and no expense has been spared in fitting and furnishing for the accommodation of pupils.

The general educational system thus far adopted is that of the latest and most approved methods.

The public schools of St. Paul are not only serving admirable educational purposes, but they of late have afforded such special proof of increase of population in the city that a few statistics on this point may be presented. Up to three years ago (when the great and sudden increase in St. Paul's population began) the ten or twelve school houses then built were not only ample to accommodate all public school scholars, but it was thought that no more buildings would be needed for several years. In the spring of 1881, however, every school was crowded beyond its proper capacity, and it was concluded to erect new buildings as quickly as possible. Among others, the large and costly Van Buren school ($35,000) was decided upon, and there was some objection to locating a building of such magnitude on the then sparsely settled Dayton's bluff. Even the school inspector for that ward argued that the edifice would amply accommodate all school purposes for the district for at least five years. Much to everybody's surprise the great building was not only crowded to the exclusion of many scholars the very next year, 1882, but in the spring of 1883 a $15,000 addition was required; and even that has failed to meet the requirements of that locality, for now a new building is to be built this season in East St. Paul. The same rate of increase has applied to every other portion of the city, so that while the school house facilities have been very nearly doubled within three years, every edifice is crowded with pupils against only partially filled rooms up to 1881. The school statistics simply prove what other statistics argue, that St. Paul's population has more than doubled within three years.

MINNESOTA'S PUBLIC SCHOOL FUND.

The public school fund of the State of Minnesota is one of the largest funds of its class. By a wise public policy in providing for future needs, two sections of land in each township of the State were set apart and dedicated to the school fund. This gives one acre of ground out of each eighteen in the entire State to the purposes of general education. The result is that the general school fund of the State now amounts to nearly $6,000,000. This vast sum will keep on increasing for many years. It is estimated that the total school fund, when the lands are disposed of, will reach $15,000,000.

PAROCHIAL AND PRIVATE SCHOOLS AND ACADEMIES.

There are twenty-four private schools and academies in St. Paul. Among these the Academy of St. Joseph is prominent, having one of the largest and most

NEW UNIVERSITY HALL, HAMLINE.

costly structures for its purposes to be found in the West.   Besides English and
classical academies, there are several first-class kindergartens, an art school, two
Lutheran schools and several German institutions.   The parochial schools are all
first-class and largely attended.

MACALESTER COLLEGE.

Just beyond the city limits west. on what is called Snelling avenue, is located
Macalester (Presbyterian) college.   The preparatory school of the college has been
long in existence in St. Paul under the style of Baldwin school; and the college is
in fact the outgrowth of the success of that institution.   The principal hall of the
new college, costing about $30,000, has just been completed, and the formal open-
ing will occur in September, 1884.   Macalester has a fund of $75,000, besides a site
of forty acres of land which has been platted into a beautiful park, and which is
worth many thousand dollars.   The college will speedily rank among the chief
institutions of learning in the State, and will afford convenient facilities for those
who desire to educate their children in a school conducted under the auspices of
the Presbyterian church.   Rev. Edward H. Neill is the president, and its trustees
comprise many of the most prominent names in Minnesota.   The college is a
delightful half-hour's drive from the center of the city, or is reached by railway in

a few minutes' run by trains that leave the St. Paul union depot every hour of the day. Letters of inquiry relative to Macalester college may be addressed to the president, St. Paul, Minn.

HAMLINE UNIVERSITY.

Hamline university (Methodist Episcopal) is located on the St. Paul, Minneapolis & Manitoba railway, just beyond the city limits of St. Paul, and is reached by hourly trains from this city in about twelve minutes. It is the oldest denominational institution of learning in Minnesota, having been chartered in 1854, and first established at Red Wing, whence it was moved to St. Paul. The building represented by the foregoing cut is the new University Hall, recently completed and dedicated in January of the present year.

The new hall is a large and commodious structure, admirably adapted to the purpose for which it is designed. The Ladies' Hall of the institution is also a fine building, and provides accommodations for sixty-five students. Between these two main buildings is situated the laboratory, well supplied with the most modern chemical and philosophical apparatus. About 135 students have been in attendance the past year. The total expense for a student for the entire year need not exceed $190. The university has an endowment (productive and unproductive) of $135,000. Information relative to Hamline university may be had by addressing Rev. Dr. G. H. Bridgman, president Hamline university, St. Paul, Minn.

NEW INSTITUTIONS PROJECTED.

The Baptists of Minnesota are contemplating the establishment of a college, and the proposed site is midway between Hamline and Macalester. The Scandinavians are also moving in the matter of removing an institution now located in Chicago to St. Paul. The Catholic church has a splendid site for a college on Lake Johanna — the front to be on Snelling avenue, upon which the colleges now established are located — and a large institution will undoubtedly soon be founded at that point.

St. Paul's Churches.

The religious inspiration to which the city is indebted for its very name, has marked the character of every era of St. Paul's development. The result is not only a city of churches — for there are seventy church edifices now built, or in process of construction — but a municipality less tainted with crime, disorder, pauperism and suffering, than most places of its population. The church edifices, as a class, are at least average structures in size and cost, while the societies, of whatever denomination, are growing and prosperous.

PRESBYTERIAN AND CONGREGATIONAL.

There are six Presbyterian and four Congregational societies, with their churches so located that every section of the residence localities is convenient to a house of worship. Several of the societies are very wealthy, and all are flourishing. As an illustration, the membership of the House of Hope society (Presbyterian) is nearly 600.

METHODIST EPISCOPAL.

The Methodist Episcopal churches number twelve, of which two are German, two Scandinavian, and one African. The leading societies have membership of

First Baptist Church

Catholic Church

from 200 to 350.   One of the principal educational institutions in the state, Hamline university, located just outside the city limits of St. Paul, is a monument to the prosperity and energy of the Methodist denomination of the State.

EPISCOPAL.

Some of the Episcopal parishes are among the oldest church organizations in the west.   The churches number eight, all wealthy and prominent among the religious societies of the city.   The leading church has about 600 communicants. The parochial schools are excellent, and are well sustained.

BAPTIST.

The Baptist organizations number six, and are among the strongest societies in the city.   The First Baptist church, with a membership of nearly 500, is one of the notable edifices of St. Paul.   There is one German Baptist church, and one colored.   The societies are all notably prosperous, and there is almost a certainty that a Baptist college will be located in this immediate vicinity this summer.

LUTHERAN.

There are no less than nine Lutheran churches, with an average membership exceeding any denomination except the Catholic.   There are four German Lutheran, two Norwegian, two Swedish, and one Danish.   The Lutherans are now negotiating for a site for a college.

CATHOLIC.

St. Paul offers exceptional advantages to Catholic residents.   There are nine Catholic churches, and one (German) in process of erection.   In four of the churches the congregation is English speaking ; in two, German ; in one, Polish ; in one, French ; and in one, Bohemian.   All of the churches except the Bohemian have parochial schools connected with them.   There are also two first-class, select, female academies in which the courses are thorough and complete.   Connected with the various churches are total abstinence, benevolent, literary and charitable societies, all in flourishing condition ; the total number of Catholic societies in St. Paul being twenty-six.   The Catholics also sustain a large hospital, under the charge of the Sisters of St. Joseph; two orphan asylums (German and English), a House of the Good Shepherd, or female reformatory; and a Home for the Aged under the direction of the Little Sisters of the Poor.   Seventeen priests minister to the spiritual needs of the Catholics of St. Paul.   Two of the churches have a membership of over 4,000 each.   Among the most widely known Catholic prelates of this country are Bishop Grace and Bishop Ireland of this city.   Catholics who desire further information in this regard than here presented, may address the editor of *North-western Chronicle*, St. Paul, Minn.

UNITARIAN.

The Unitarians have a beautiful church edifice and a large, flourishing society. No organization was perfected here until 1872, but since that time it has made rapid advancement.

EVANGELICAL.

There are three Evangelical churches and one United Evangelical, all well sustained.

HEBREW.

There are two Hebrew congregations, and a fine synagogue was completed in 1882.   The congregations are wealthy and the societies prosperous.

SWEDENBORGIAN.

This faith is represented by one society, which was organized in 1873.

BENEVOLENT AND CHARITABLE SOCIETIES.

There are a number of important benevolent and charitable societies, other than those mentioned in the summary of Catholic institutions above given.   The

Protestant Orphan Asylum was organized in 1865 and is conducted by a number of the wealthiest ladies of the city. It is a model institution of its class. St. Luke's Hospital is sustained by the Episcopal church, and is an institution of recognized service by all classes of citizens. There is a well-managed Swedish hospital at Lake Como. One of the most meritorious institutions in St. Paul is the Woman's Christian Home. The Home for the Friendless and the Magdalen Home are two institutions which are accomplishing more of good than could well be expressed in the limits of these pages. In this connection should be mentioned the temperance work of Bishop Grace and Bishop Ireland. The world is familiar with the general work in this direction of these distinguished prelates, but it cannot know how much has been accomplished for St. Paul. The notable rarity of burglaries, night assaults and crime generally in this city is believed to be largely due to the organization and maintenance of temperance societies, which have made sc res of persons prosperous citizens, who might otherwise have been reduced to law-breaking in any of its countless forms.

All in all, the religious and moral influences of St. Paul are of a character to satisfy the most prudent and consciencious.

Remarkable Increase in Population.

Statistics of increase in population are more readily applied, as a rule, in forming an estimate of a city's growth, than are figures relating to general business development. The reader's attention is therefore directed particularly to subjoined statements, which are, in every instance, taken from official sources. To begin with, the population of St. Paul increased more than 100 per cent between the summer of 1880 and the spring of 1883, or in less than three years. The United States census for 1880 placed the number of inhabitants in St. Paul at 41,498, while the city directory of that year gave 16,399 names. The directory for 1883 contained 35,351 names, or 2,553 more than double the number of 1880, so that the actual per cent of increase in the three years was a fraction over 112 per cent. Upon this showing it is unhesitatingly declared that St. Paul has established a record of growth in population which has never been equaled by a city of similar size in the history of this country. At this time the publishers of the city directory are canvassing for the issue of 1884, and from them it is learned that the ratio of increase which marked 1881 and 1882 was fully maintained during the past year, and that the forthcoming volume will demonstrate beyond any possibility of doubt that the population of St. Paul is now considerably more than 100,-000. However, the estimates of population here given, in order to be entirely within bounds, will be made upon the basis of the directory of last year. To reiterate, the number of names in the directory for 1883 was 35,351. In Chicago, Cincinnati, Cleveland, Buffalo and Kansas City the multiple 3½ is used in determining population from number of names in respective directories. On this basis the population of St. Paul would be 123,728. This multiple, however, is believed to be too large, especially for western cities, and so the conservative rule adopted by Milwaukee, Indianapolis, Denver, etc., is here used. The towns last named apply the multiple three, and on the same basis of calculation St. Paul has a population of 106,053. With the usual conservatism of the people of the city, the general rule, when speaking upon this subject, is to place the number in even figures, at 100,000. It must be borne in mind, however, that these calculations are on the basis of data secured almost a year ago, and it is certain that the actual population of the city now exceeds the figures given.

COMPARISONS WITH OTHER CITIES.

In the endeavor to realize the recent wonderful growth of St. Paul, comparison with the increase in population of other cities will serve a purpose. For instance, the increase in names in the St. Paul directory for 1883 over 1882 was 1,610 more than the increase in Chicago for the same time. In other words, St. Paul added 4,800 more to its population than did Chicago, notwithstanding the disparity in size of the two cities. If this ratio of increase is compared with relative population, it will be seen that St. Paul's gain is many hundred per cent greater than that of Chicago.

Inasmuch as this phenomenal development has occurred within three years — for previous to 1880 the city's growth was hardly up to the average of western towns — it is impossible to calculate what the result in the immediate future will be. It is pretty certain, however, that the remarkable ratio will continue right along for several years, at least, as it is not at all in excess of requirements that will be made, from this time forward, upon the acknowledged metropolis of the equally developing region between St. Paul and the Pacific coast. Present indications, indeed, are that the influx of population this season will be greater than ever before.

GROWTH BY YEARS.

The following figures will afford information concerning the growth of population by decades up to 1880, and the subsequent increase by years:

Year.	No. Inhabitants.
1850*	840
1860	10,600
1870*	20,300
1880*	41,498
1881	50,900
1882	75,835
18 3	106,053

* United States census.

River Traffic.

From the middle of April to the middle of November, or more than one-half the year, St. Paul enjoys uninterrupted steamboat communication with all towns on the lower Mississippi. * No less than seventeen steamboats ply regularly on the lines out of St. Paul. This traffic is now steadily increasing, and when the great reservoir system, now being constructed by the government, on the head-waters of the river, is completed, it will, by affording a steady guard against exceptionally low water, largely stimulate the carrying trade of the water route. The steamers of the St. Paul lines are largely patronized by passengers during the summer, and afford the most pleasant means of journeying for tourists and summer resort patrons. The river route will ever protect St. Paul from any possible form of freight-carrying extortion. It is also believed that the day will soon come when a fair portion of the wheat product of the Northwest will find cheap transportation to European markets via the river to New Orleans, and thence by ocean vessels to Liverpool.

In addition to the Mississippi river navigation, steamers ply from St. Paul to St. Croix river points, thus tapping the pineries of Northeastern Minnesota and Northwestern Wisconsin.

Navigation of the Minnesota river, which empties into the Mississippi just above this city, is practicable, and by means of which the very interior of the state is reached; but railway facilities are so complete that the services of the Minnesota are not called into requisition.

* The ice moved out of the river this year, 1883, March 26.

A ST. PAUL HOME. — RESIDENCE OF COMMODORE N. W. KITTSON, CORNER SUMMIT AND DAYTON AVENUES. BUILT OF CUT KASOTA STONE. COST, EXCLUSIVE OF GROUNDS, $150,000.

Building Review.

The number and value of new buildings erected in St. Paul during the past two years and projected for the season of 1884 may be taken as one of the most positive proofs of the recent marvelous development of the metropolis of the North-west. Three years ago the building improvements in this city were not of importance enough to be alloted space in the annual report of the Bradstreet Commercial Agency; yet in that concern's building review for the third quarter of 1883, St. Paul is given fourth place among American cities in the amount of money expended in new buildings — New York, Chicago and Cincinnati leading in the order named. The figures, however, in detail, are of most interest and importance.

BRADSTREET'S REPORT.

Bradstreet says: "The order in which the cities ranked (so far as reported) during eight months in 1883, based on the gross amounts expended by each in building, is shown as follows:

New York	$37,207,112	Kansas City	$ 2,000,000
Chicago	12,780,000	Grand Rapids	2,000,000
Cincinnati	11,000,000	Toledo	1,490,000
St. Paul	9,580,000	Pittsburg	1,420,000
Minneapolis	8,310,000	Memphis	1,300,000
Cleveland	3,750,000	Indianapolis	1,250,000
New Orleans	3,000,000	Burlington	1,100,000
Denver	3,000,000	Milwaukee	1,070,000
Des Moines	2,750,000	Nashville	1,050,000
Detroit	2,580,000		

ANALYSIS OF THE FIGURES.

The town, then, which three years ago was unimportant to Bradstreet's report, now expends annually three-fourths as much money in upbuilding as Chicago, presses closely upon the energy of Cincinnati, and completely overshadows Cleveland and New Orleans by more than three-fold. Milwaukee, Indianapolis, Nashville, Pittsburg and other reputed prosperous and growing cities sink into positive insignificance in the light of Bradstreet's report. Significant as the above figures are, they do not tell the full story of St. Paul's building growth, for the reason that the marked development in this line has not been confined to a portion, merely, of 1883, but began in 1881, continued in 1882, increased to the splendid results of 1883, and bids fair to eclipse all previous work in the present season of 1884.

RECENT BUILDING GROWTH.

Up to the beginning of 1881, St. Paul's upbuilding naturally kept pace with its steady but not rapid growth in other ways. Then came, or rather began, that remarkable general development which in three years doubled the population of the city. The year 1881 scored a total of 1,161 buildings erected, of which 1,000 were residences, and the total cost was $4,571,700; while the past year surpassed that record by about 200 per cent. The tabulated statement will illustrate:

YEAR.	No. Business Houses.	No. Residences.	Public Buildings.	Total No. Buildings.	Aggregate Cost.
1881	139	1,009	13	1,161	$4,571,700
1882	234	2,178	29	2,481	8,399,000
1883	434	3,124	49	3,607	11,938,950

It will be seen by the figures presented that St. Paul has, within three years, erected 807 business houses, 91 public buildings, and 6,302 residences—a total of 7,209 structures—at an aggregate cost of $24,909,650. If figures ever "speak for themselves," they certainly do in this instance. They prove conclusively that St. Paul is growing more rapidly (in proportion) than any other city in the country; for while three cities lead this in actual building expenditure, the ratio of increase in building operations for the year as compared with the preceding season, is several times greater in St. Paul than in any one of its rivals. Remarkable as this building growth has been it has not kept pace with the actual living and business requirements of the incoming population, for there is all the time an unsupplied demand for houses and business places. The present season of 1884 has opened with even greater building activity than characterized the season of 1883, and architects and builders agree that this will be a much more important building year than any St. Paul has ever known. There are now in process of construction a very large number of splendid business blocks; and the cost of those now building—to say nothing of those projected, and upon which work will begin this year—will be upward of $3,000,000. From work now in progress architects and builders believe that the building record of 1884 will aggregate at least $13,000,000.

CHARACTER OF BUSINESS BLOCKS.

The general style and size of business blocks that have been erected in St. aul within the past two years, would do credit to the architecture of the best uilt city in the country. Nearly all of the large number of blocks built in the usiness district since 1881 have been five stories in height, and finished, both ithin and without, in costly style and most approved modern adaptations to the articular uses of the structure, whether for wholesale, retail or apartment puroses. Anything less than a $50,000 structure is now deemed of little importance, hile many blocks costing from $100,000 to $250,000 have been built, or are in me stage of progress. All of the business blocks now building are faced with he finest pressed brick obtainable, while trimmings are of terra cotta and different inds of stone found in Minnesota, including granite, Kasota sandstone, Fond du ac (purple) sandstone, or jasper from Sioux Falls. The illustrations presented of usiness houses will give a correct idea of the class of buildings built recently in his city. At the present time the most important structure in process of contruction is the Hotel Ryan, to cost $1,000,000. The aggregate street frontage of usiness blocks erected during 1883, or now in process of erection, is over two iiles.

PRIVATE RESIDENCES.

St. Paul has for many years ranked as "a wealthy city" in the sense that it as very many capitalists in proportion to population. It is, therefore, to be xpected that it should even now be a place of palatial residences. It may surrise the general reader to learn that $15,000 to $20,000 mansions are quite comion in St. Paul, yet such is the fact, while many are now building to cost from 30,000 to $75,000 each. A view of the residence of Commodore Kittson is preented as a means of identifying the general style of the best class of Summit venue (the most select residence street) homes. The edifice, exclusive of grounds, st $150,000. ' However, it is in the general character of medium houses that St. aul attracts most favorable comment from visitors, who are invariably surprised find the most compactly built residence portion, St. Anthony hill, to be covered ith dwellings ranging in cost from $5,000 to $15,000, exclusive of grounds.

In general, visitors admit that St. Paul is a splendidly built city thus far; nd residents know that there is marked improvement in this regard year by year. he recently built portion of town, whether business or residence, will compare vorably with the best work in modern cities.

Real Estate.

Real estate for several years prior to 1881, had been entirely inactive in St. aul, and as a natural consequence the great bulk of realty was owned by residents, peculators having quitted the market years before. The result of this has been hat long-time residents have profited by the recent rise in values and have been ble, by releasing a portion of their holdings, to make improvements that could ot otherwise have been made. This accounts in great degree for the enormous p-building that has been carried on during the past three years. The increase in roperty values has simply made St. Paul owners several times richer than they ere in 1880. Every dollar invested by capitalists, or expended in the purchase a lot for business or residence purposes, has simply augmented by so much the orking or improvement capital of the city. While the city's growth has been ally wonderful, real estate values have never reached the "boom" condition which has ruined so many small western towns. All along there has been a conservative policy on the part of business men generally, which has militated against undue excitement in this line. The consequence is that realty values are yet much lower in St. Paul than in most cities of its size, to say nothing of its prospects. Indeed, realty holders have not as yet discounted the future. Actual prices, however will best illustrate. Property within a block and a half of the new $1,000,-000 hotel can be bought for less than $225 per front foot; property on Fifth and Sixth streets, in what is properly the wholesale district, can be had at from $175 to $300 per front foot; the very best vacant property in St. Paul can be bought for $500 per front foot; residence lots in the choicest district of the city, 50x175 feet, can be had at from $1,600 to $2,500; lots 40x125 in districts where workingmen have located are plenty at from $175 to $300; good residence lots in medium districts range from $400 to $1,000. Outlying business lots, on Seventh street, Rice street, or other thoroughfares leading out of the city, may be had from $600 to $1,500. Acre property, adjoining the city limits, is held at $200 to $1,000 per acre. Within four or five miles of the city good land may be bought for $50 per acre, while first-class lands for garden or farming purposes within ten or twelve miles of the city may be had at from $20 to $25 per acre. These prices are cheap, considering St. Paul's present development, and are certainly worth the attention of capitalists who can comprehend the future possibilities of this city and the Northwest. There is no other city of equal size and evident prospects where real estate is so low priced. The field of investment is fertile, and will yield large returns. Business for the present year promises to equal, if not surpass, that of last year, when the aggregate sales amounted to $12,981,331. Compared with 1882 the statistics of sales are as follows:

	No. Deeds.	Consideration.
1883	4,874	$12,981,331
1882	1,447	9,354,841
Increase in 1883	427	$ 3,626,490

In this connection, it should be stated that there is no speculating in St. Paul in what are termed option contracts; a species of real estate gambling common in some Northwestern cities. It is also to be noted that property is not heavily mortgaged. Taxes are light, for the reason that assessed values are very low in comparison with actual selling prices.

Health of St. Paul.

Invalids in search of health find it in St. Paul, if relief to their individual ailment is to be discovered in this world. Those who have never suffered illness or disease are equally interested in vital statistics which suggest a locality where immunity may be longest enjoyed. Recent official reports prove that this is the healthiest city on the continent, but they do not explain why St. Paul is so comparatively free from disease and death. It is now universally known that perfect drainage is one of the best guarantees of good health to the people of a large city. In this respect the site of St. Paul may be said to be perfect, for there is not a district of the city that does not enjoy natural drainage. This has enabled engineers to perfect a sewer system which is unsurpassed by that of any other place. How free from the objections that pertain to the sewerage of cities built upon a plain, the St. Paul system is, it may be mentioned that in a population of 100,000 there were only 22 cases of diphtheria during 1883 along the sewer lines of the city. Good sewerage gives health to large centers of population, and that of St.

Paul is absolutely perfect. The elevation of all parts of the city above the river insures for time to come easy disposition of the sewage, no matter to what extent population may increase. So far as climate is concerned, its salubrity is famous the world over. The atmosphere is as dry as that of mountainous regions, without the rarity of great elevations which induce heart disease and nervous complications. Physicians have for many years advised St. Paul residence for persons suffering from pulmonary disease, and the efficacy of the prescription is attested by thousands of improved cases. Strangers visiting St. Paul invariably note the health-glowing complexions of young people who have grown up here from birth or childhood. It is the result of dry, pure atmosphere and absence of malaria. The dryness of atmosphere is illustrated by the fact that it is difficult to make new arrivals from the south or east, in winter time, believe that they experience cold 10° or 15° below zero when the mercury demonstrates that such a degree really exists: for that degree of cold is not so uncomfortable here as zero would be in the lake or seacoast regions. In general terms, so far as cold is concerned, the average winter weather at St. Paul is far more comfortable than that of Boston, New York or Chicago. Another advantage St. Paul enjoys is the purity of its water supply: the city water being taken from a group of lakes that are in fact a series of gigantic springs.

STATISTICS.

On this point, however, the reader will naturally desire to consider official statistics. By those presented it will be seen that St. Paul is without a rival:

Average annual death-rate per 1,000 inhabitants of leading American cities for the year 1883:

St. Paul	11.72	Boston	23.10
Milwaukee	19.30	Baltimore	25.25
Cincinnati	19.50	New York	25.30
Chicago	20.70	New Orleans	34.83
Philadelphia	21.70	Average death rate the world over	22.00
San Francisco	20.80		

This showing is altogether satisfactory, yet it is unjust to St. Paul's almost perfect healthfulness in that the rate is increased here by the deaths of many invalids who seek recuperation, when they are at death's door before they conclude to try this locality.

It should be noted particularly that, by reason of its perfect drainage St. Paul is comparatively free from fevers of a typhoid character that have at times pervaded neighborhoods that are so situated as to make it impossible to secure proper sewerage.

The General Climate of Minnesota.

The fact that Eastern and Southern physicians recommend their patients who are afflicted with pulmonary symptoms to "try the climate of Minnesota" is evidence enough of the salubrity of atmosphere characteristic of the State. The chief merit of Minnesota's atmosphere is its dryness, which precludes the pestilential "muggy" heat of more southern latitudes, or the chilling cold of the lake and ocean region. This freedom from moisture does not come from rarity of the atmosphere, so fatal to persons who have a tendency to heart difficulties or disease, but is due to the prevailing winds, which, coming from the west, do not have opportunity to gather dampness from passage over a large body of water. The result is that the actual mercurial temperature of either summer or winter does not convey to the Eastern or Southern resident anything like a correct idea of the effect of that temperature upon humanity, animal or even vegetable life. For instance, a temperature of 98° in midsummer would not be so oppressive in St. Paul as 90° would be in Chicago, as a point in the lake region, or New York, as a point on the Atlantic. On the other hand, a temperature of 20° below zero in Minnesota in winter would not inconvenience a person or animal so much as zero would in any of the Middle or Eastern States; that is, if it were possible to subject a person to a temperature of zero in New York, at the next moment subject him to a test of 20° below zero in St. Paul, the individual so tested would undoubtedly say that he felt less discomfort in the St. Paul temperature. There is so little dampness in the atmosphere of this region that there is no chilling effect even in the very coldest weather experienced. Animals bear abundant evidence of the salubrity of this climate, for they are seldom or never seen to shiver as they do in places where the air is laden with moisture. People who come here from the East, where great care is exercised to prevent vegetables freezing in cellars in the winter time, are invariably surprised, after noting the degree of cold registered by their thermometer, to find that their cellars are warm and their winter stores safe. The reason of this is that the cold is not, to use the popular expression, penetrating; that is, there is no moisture-burdened cold to work its way through the very stones, and blast everything with its chilling breath. It is maintained, therefore, and the action of physicians in sending patients here to recuperate is proof of it, that the average winter climate of Minnesota is not so severe as that of the Eastern States. So far as what is termed "pleasant weather" is concerned, St. Paul and Minnesota may safely challenge comparison with any section of the Union. To illustrate, spring opens with bright, clear, warm days about the first or tenth of April. The sun shines, the air is balmy, and one feels that he is safe from the very possibility of death-dealing fogs and marrow-chilling mists. There has been no gradual breaking up of winter with alternate sleet, hail or snow, but a sudden transition it almost seems (strangers invariably comment upon this) from bracing winter weather to growing spring time. Anything like what is termed a "wet spell" in the East or South is almost unknown. From the time spring opens one is assured of delightful weather — the spring and summer rains are never protracted — until past the middle of November (and often far into December), the last few weeks of fall being termed "Indian summer" and providing the most exquisitely delightful days imaginable. When winter assumes control it is done quickly, and here again the transition is marked. But winter in St. Paul does not signify daily and hourly dribblings of snow and sleet, but clear, crisp days with bright sunshine, and nights of moonlight and starlight such as are never dreamed of in atmospheres surcharged with dampness. Cold weather, then, does not count against pleasurable existence, but favors it as compared with the changeable temperature and degrees of humidity of Southern latitudes and Eastern longitudes. In other words the winter climate is even, free from rain, and is advantageous every way to health, labor and business. It is desired particularly to call the attention of artisans and workingmen to the fact that owing to the few rainy days of summer and the few blustering days of winter, that in all out-of-doors pursuits a larger number of days can be put in during the year than in most other localities.

The summer months are voted "perfect" by the large and yearly increasing throng of summer visitors, who now frequent the fashionable resorts in St. Paul and vicinity; and if these same visitors would remain through the glories of one Indian summer and the health-giving months of a bright, crisp, invigorating winter, they would be unwilling to give up residence here for the mud, slop and chills of their own less favored localities.

So far as general healthfulness of climate is concerned, the fact that St. Paul's death-rate for the past year was but 11.65 per 1,000 of population against 24.36 for New York and 22 for the world's average, is sufficient to indicate the spot where health may be regained and long life enjoyed.

HOTEL RYAN, CORNER ROBERT AND SIXTH STREETS.

The above cut represents the great hotel now in process of erection in St. Paul. When completed it will be one of the most costly and imposing structures of its class in America, and will far exceed in elegance, size and cost any hotel building north or west of Chicago. The elevation above presented consists of 225 feet frontage on Sixth street and 150 feet on Robert. It will be seven stories high and of modern Gothic style of architecture and ornamentation. The cost will exceed $1,000,000. It is being built by Mr. Dennis Ryan, one of St. Paul's wealthiest citizens. In addition to the structure above represented, Mr. Ryan will build a vast edifice on the Seventh street front of the same block, which will be connected with the hotel proper, and will become, in fact, a part of the grand structure.

Suburban Attractions.

St. Paul and its suburbs will eventually become as delightful a residence locality as may be found in the country. It is difficult to picture in the imagination a more charming combination of river, hill, lake and forest than exists in fact at innumerable points of observation within a radius of ten or twelve miles from the business center of the city. The average visitor to St. Paul notices the majestic expanse of river and the terraced highlands that encircle the city, views Fort Snelling with the awe incident to historical association, looks with pleased surprise upon the beauties of Minnehaha Falls, and votes the Capital City and its surroundings surpassingly beautiful. Yet the visitor has seen absolutely nothing of those landscape attractions which are one day to make the suburbs of St. Paul more delightful than those of any other American city.

The accompanying map will illustrate the reason of the above assertion. By it the reader will observe that the country immediately north of St. Paul is fairly a net-work of lovely lakes. In every dimple of prairie, in every depression of woodland is set a crystal gem that in any other locality would be considered an invaluable addition to the surrounding landscape. The district outlined by the map is all within the suburbs proper of St. Paul, the northern limit being just ten miles from the corporate limits of the city. All of the lakes here indicated are of great beauty of outline and surroundings, of purest water, connected with each other by rapid running brooks, and finally finding outlet to the Mississippi river. Irregular contour of coast lines of every variety of surface—here a gentle, wooded, slope, there a bold cliff, or again a grassy vale — contribute to the exquisite beauty of these lakes. Not one in all the number but presents many perfect residence sites, locations that combine natural groves, gravel or sand beach and almost any desired land surface. All of these waters teem with fish (black and silver bass especially), are clear and cold, and from forty to sixty feet deep in their deepest parts. No large city on the continent has such a delightful suburban district.

THE LAKE DISTRICT.

That visitors—and many thousands of St. Paul's citizens who have recently located here and have not yet familiarized themselves with the beautiful surroundings—may gain some idea of Nature s free-hand distribution of favors hereabouts, a brief glance at the lakes that lie within ten miles of the city limits may be had. One can scarcely get out of the built-up portion of the city, in any direction save directly westward, until the gleam of lovely waters is seen near at hand. Driving northwesterly from the business center and before the city limits are reached we arrive at Lake Como, one mile long and from one-fourth to half-a-mile wide. About this lake the city has established a beautiful park of two hundred and sixty acres. One and one-half miles west of Como are Rock and Horseshoe lakes, both small, but adding beauty to the landscape. One and one-half miles north of Como is Bennett's lake, a pleasant spot, and one-half mile east of this Owasso, a beautiful body of water one half mile wide and one and one-half long, the seat of several summer homes. Just beyond Owasso is Lake Josephine, a perfect gem, surrounded by a number of fine cottages. Half-a-mile northwest of Josephine is Lake Johanna. a nearly round lake about one-mile in diameter, and one of the best fishing resorts. On this lake will be erected the new Catholic college, to front on the continuation of Snelling avenue, on which (as shown in the map) are already located Hamline university (Methodist), and Macalester college (Presbyterian). One mile southwest of Johanna is Wilson's lake, then follow Poplar, Round, and Long lakes. We have then, in a drive of ten miles in a northwesterly direction, discovered eleven beautiful lakes.

Starting again from St. Paul and driving directly north out Rice street, McCarron's and Sandy lakes are reached in three miles. Next comes Lake Savage, about which clusters "St. John City," a French hamlet older than St. Paul. A little to the west is seen Owasso again, but directly north is Vadnais lake, a considerable body of water of low temperature and purest quality, from which St. Paul is taking its water supply. One-half mile northeast of Vadnais is Lambert's lake, one mile broad, then Sucker and Grass lakes. We now arrive at a cluster of exceedingly beautiful bodies of water called respectively Pleasant lake, Charles lake, Turtle lake, Marsden's lake and Lake Gilfillan. Not more than half-a-mile intervens between any two of these romantic lakes, and all of them are in full view from many of the high points between them. On Pleasant lake the president of the St. Paul and Manitoba railway, J. J. Hill, has purchased three thousand acres of ground for a summer home and a fancy stock farm. The place is to be

Scale. 2½ miles to the inch

The above map represents the lake district about St. Paul Fort Snelling, Minnehaha Falls, and the sites of Hamline University and Macalester College.

improved by the outlay of many thousands of dollars. On Turtle lake, three-fourths of a mile from Pleasant lake, Commodore Kittson has his summer place. The drive to this point is less than fourteen miles, but in that distance fourteen lakes have been passed.

Starting for the third time from St. Paul and driving a little east of north, Lake Phalen is met with just outside the city limits; the lake from which beautiful Phalen creek carries all the surplus waters of the lake district to outlet in the Mississippi. Then come Spoon, Gervais (very pretty), Kohlman's, Fitzhugh's, Rice and Goose lakes, all well stocked with fish and affording innumerable lovely sites for summer homes. Now we reach that splendid body of water which is the pride of St. Paul,

WHITE BEAR LAKE.

Here, upon the most beautiful of all Northwestern lakes, are the summer cottages of many of the wealthiest residents of the city. It is the seat of four hotels, which are all fashionable resorts, the popular camping ground of the State militia of Minnesota and the annual meeting place of the Mahtomedi Assembly. The shores of White Bear seem to have been treated by Nature in a masterly attempt at landscape gardening. In all the twenty or more miles of shore line there is scarcely a foot that is not perfect for residence grounds. The waters are clear, deep, very cold, and abound in endless variety of fish. White Bear is ten miles by railway (St. Paul & Duluth) from St. Paul, and numerous trains make it a convenient as well as delightful summer residence. White Bear is not only a favorite retreat for St. Paul people, but its hotels are thronged with visitors from the East and South during the season, and it is now recognized as one of the most fashionable of all the Northwestern summer resorts.

Within one mile, to the northeast, of White Bear is Bald Eagle, a lake nearly as large and beautiful, also reached by rail, and rapidly becoming a popular resort. Birch, Otter, Wilkinson's, Amelia, Big Tree lake, Long lake, Lake DeMontieville and Lake Jane are pretty sheets of water in this same district, making sixteen in all passed in a trip of twelve miles on this route out of St. Paul.

To the east of the city, within a short distance, are Beaver, Elmo, Frost's, Wakefield's and Silver lakes, all beautiful and being rapidly utilized for summer residence purposes. Tanner's, Fish and several smaller lakes lie to the southeast of the city. Crossing the Mississippi river and driving directly south, many lakes are found, chief of which in beauty is Thoreau, already occupied as a summer home.

The map also indicates the location of Fort Snelling and Minnehaha falls, either of which may be reached in a few minutes by rail (many times a day) or by one of the most beautiful drives possible to imagine. Both places are also reached by pleasure steamers, which ply during the season of navigation.

LAKE MINNETONKA.

There is still another attractive place to be included in St. Paul's suburbs, and which is reached in less than an hour's ride by rail from this city. Reference is made to Lake Minnetonka, rapidly becoming one of the most popular and widely known summer resorts in the entire North. Here is found a lake of surpassing beauty, with great steamers plying its waters and its shores affording hotel facilities that are not surpassed by those of the favorite sea-beach resorts in the neighborhood of New York. In fact, the Hotel Lafayette, built by St. Paul capital, is one of the largest edifices of its class in the world. The accompanying view is a perfect representation of the great hotel and its surroundings. Trains run hourly during the season from St. Paul to Lake Minnetonka. It is only within two years that the facilities at Minnetonka met the requirements of summer visitors, but now the resort has no superior in general conveniences and attractions. It is now the best patronized resort in the Northwest, and its number of summer visitors will continue to increase yearly as its advantages are more widely known and appreciated.

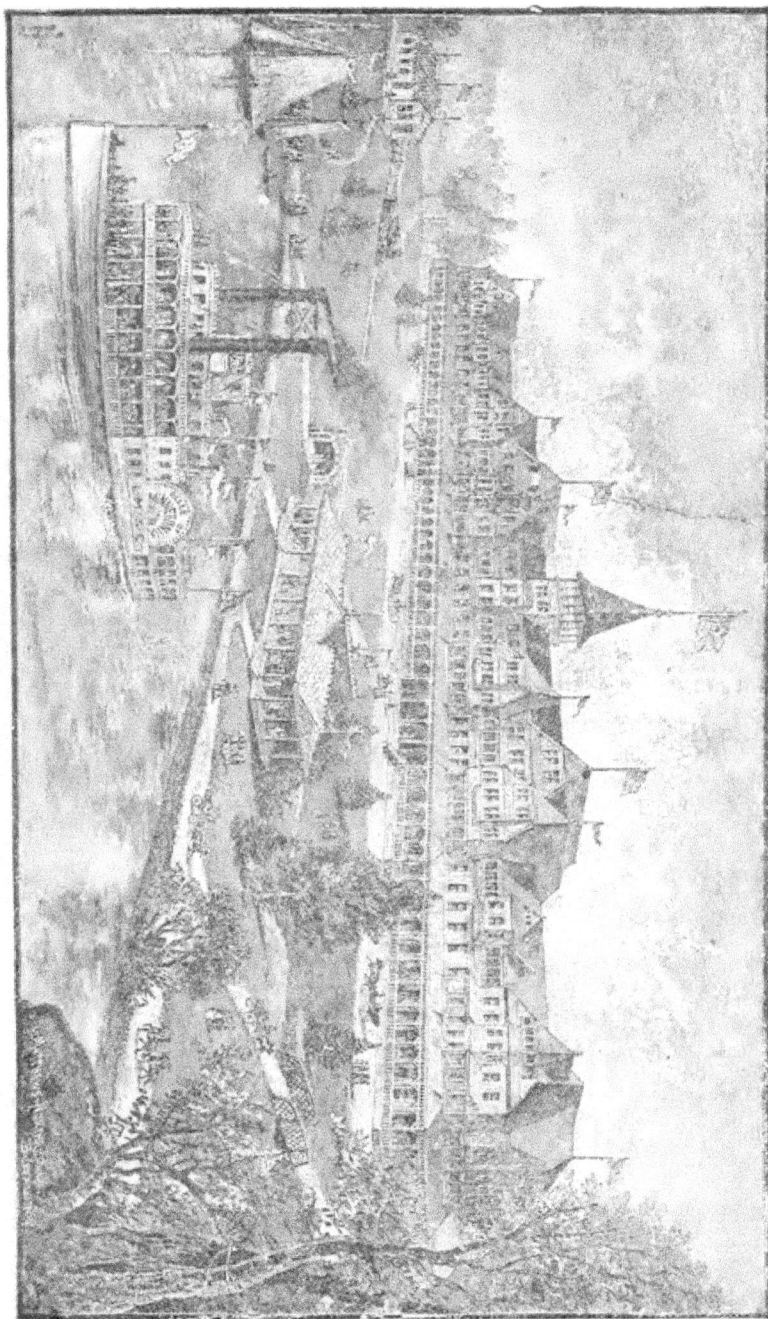

HOTEL LAFAYETTE, LAKE MINNETONKA

Who so blind that they cannot see the advantage of such surroundings as rea above indicated to a great commercial center? No American city of importance has equal suburban attractions. Unlike the river and coast regions about New York, there is no malaria in this exquisite lake district. It is simply a summer paradise of invigorating atmosphere, pure water and unsurpassed beauties of land-scape, combining pleasures of society, boating, bathing, hunting and fishing.

Cost of Living in St. Paul.

Upon this subject the information given has been gathered with greatest care, that persons of moderate means may be able to determine positively what their living expenses will be, upon the basis of average prices for all kinds of family requirements, if they conclude to move to St. Paul.

Rents—Good, eight-room houses within ten minutes walk of the business portion of town average $30 per month if supplied with city water. Three story new and elegant brick residences of twelve rooms, all modern conveniences of water, bath, furnace, etc., are now (March 15) on the market at $58 per month. Fair six-room houses (new) within twelve minutes walk of the Union depot rent for $15 per month. Workingmen's cottages in West St. Paul or in the out-lying districts range from $8 to $12 per month. Rooms in the heart of the city are proportionately high, but may be had in desirable blocks at from $10 to $25. Neat seven or eight-room dwellings in the best portion of the residence districts range from $25 to $45 per month. Houses are scarce, but thousands of new ones are built each season so that the supply is kept just about equal to the demand, and there is therefore no extortion in the matter of rents.

Fuel—The best seasoned hard maple wood may be bought delivered at $6.00 per cord. Oak and other hard woods are proportionately cheaper; mixed oak and elm $3.75. The best nut coal is now, delivered, $10 per ton, but may be con-tracted in the fall for about $9.25. Soft coals, however, are cheap in this city, the supply coming from Iowa and Illinois. Prices range from $4 to $7.50, accord-ing to quality. Those who prefer wood to coal will note that the former fuel is cheaper here than in Eastern cities—nearly enough so to offset the difference in price of hard coal.

Servants—Serving girls are scarce and command high wages, which range from $1.50 to $4.50 per week.

Meats— Prices, retail, are taken from market reports for March 16, 1884 :

Beef—Roasting pieces, 18c; porterhouse steak, 18@20c; sirloin steak, 18c, round, 15c; chuck, 12½c; boiling pieces, 7@10c; dried beef, 18@20c. Pork—Steak and roasting pieces, 12½@15c; sausages, 10@12½c per lb.; ham, 15c; sliced do., 20c; bacon, 12½@15c; head cheese, 10@12½c. Veal—cutlets, 20c; roasting pieces, 15@18c. Mutton—Leg, 15c; stew, 5@6c; chops,12½@15c.

Groceries and Flour—Sugar, 8½ to 10 cents per pound : coffee, 13½ to 40 cents : butter, 18 to 35 cents; milk, 6 cents per quart; flour, wheat, $3 to $3.75 per 100 pounds : rye, 5 cents per pound.

Vegetables—In the fall, when vegetables are usually stored for winter, pota-toes are usually from 25 to 35 cents per bushel : cabbages, 3 to 5 cents per head ; other vegetables at proportionate prices.

From the above prices, at present ruling in this city, the reader will be able to judge very closely of the cost of living in St. Paul as compared with the local-ity in which he may at present reside.

ALLEN, MOON & CO.'S BUILDING ON THIRD STREET, IN THE WHOLESALE DISTRICT.

Postoffice Statistics.

The growth of postoffice business in St. Paul is an excellent criterion to go by in forming an estimate of the general development of the city, inasmuch as all statistics given are from official sources. The latest report of the postmaster general shows that the business transacted by the St. Paul postoffice is a good per cent larger than that of any other city of the same size in the country; a certain indication of the comparative commercial importance of the city. The following official figures will give abundant information on this point:

GROWTH OF POSTOFFICE BUSINESS — GROSS YEARLY INCOME.

1875.................$58,922.63	1878.................$63,927.59	1881.................$128,156.45
1876.................57,092.85	1879.................81,299.9	1882.................173,131.31
1877.................58,412.82	1880.................102,450.33	1883.................190,907.36

MONEY ORDER BUSINESS.

1875.................$1,254,037.00	1878.................$1,853,613.35	1881.................$3,679,525.17
1876.................1,236,409.81	1879.................2,517,523.91	1882.................4,018,241.33
1877.................1,433,969.79	1880.................2,893,695.40	1883.................4,071,303.90

Recently the fast mail service from New York to Chicago and St. Paul has been successfully inaugurated; and the fact that the service was extended to this city is proof of the importance the business world attaches to this commercial center.

A Word to Workingmen.

Any man, or woman, who has willing hands, will find work to do in St. Paul at fair wages. A great city is now building, and artizans and laborers of every class and trade are in constant demand. It is not merely that so many brick blocks and so many houses are to be erected, but a vast amount of public work in grading streets, building water works, constructing sewers, making sidewalks, etc., etc., is going on as rapidly as workmen can be secured to do the labor. Still further, every new firm that establishes business must afford employment of some sort to common labor. In fact, there was a scarcity of mechanics and laborers last year, and there will be this. Good wages obtain here — better than in Eastern and Southern cities. So far as weather interference with out-door work is concerned, the workingman can put in a greater number of days during the year in St. Paul than he can in St. Louis or Chicago. This assertion is based upon the fact that there are but few rainy days in this locality as compared with the number in either Eastern or Southern places. So far as winter weather is concerned, the average is not nearly so disagreeable and severe as in localities farther south, where the atmosphere is not so dry as it is here. All classes of workingmen now living in St. Paul are prosperous, and a very large percentage are owners of their homes. There will be a great demand for labor this season, and a sober, industrious man need not be without work a day after his arrival in St. Paul.

There is a large and of course constantly increasing demand for servant girls, and this class are paid high wages.

Building and Loan Associtions.

There are twenty-six building and loan associations in St. Paul, representing a capital of about $10,000,000, having a membership of about five thousand persons — men, women and children — and disbursing monthly from $40,000 to $50,000 in cash to members, to enable them to build houses, pay debts, or for any other purposes. These associations, in the year 1882, through their members, built three hundred houses, besides making loans for other purposes. For 1883 the statistics have not been accurately computed, but it is safe to estimate four hundred houses as the number built — worth about $300,000. The Building societies do not build houses, but loan the money to any man who can give security to pay monthly for the loan in installments about equal to what the rent of the house built would be; so that any person having a lot can mortgage the lot to the association, together with the house he is to build, with a policy of insurance assigned, and receive the money as the building progresses. The sum advanced is generally about half or two-thirds the value of the lot and insured value of the house combined. It costs about $15 per month for a loan of $1,000, principal and interest, and at the same rate for larger or smaller sums. Real estate owners are liberal in furnishing lumber and lots on monthly payments and long time, so that there is very little difficulty experienced among mechanics, clerks and others of moderate means in securing homes of their own in St. Paul at a monthly rate not

Court House & the Post Office.

exceeding rent, which homes will enhance in value, and probably be worth many times their cost long before they are paid for, if judiciously built and located. These building associations are making St. Paul in the West what Philadelphia has been in the East—"the City of Homes"—and are by no means the least of the attractions which make this city the popular resort it is for all who are seeking to better their condition in life.

Increase in Value of Realty.

Increase in value of realty, as determined by official assessment, presents the most accurate figures relative to the actual upbuilding of a city. The corporate limits of St. Paul to-day are precisely those of 1881, yet the official valuation of real property has increased 33 per cent. This remarkable increase is not due to any "boom" or fictitious advance in land values, for there are large portions of the city where the ground has appreciated but slightly since 1881, but is the result of improvements that have been made. The official figures, as given by the county auditor, are:

OFFICIAL VALUATION OF REAL PROPERTY IN ST. PAUL,

Year.	Valuation.
1881	$21,596,326
1882	30,345,072
1883	31,623,378

In considering statistics of assessed value, however, it must be borne in mind that property is generally listed at from one-third to one-half its actual market value. In St. Paul, the assessed value is more than one-third but less than one-half real value — probably about two-fifths. On this basis, the actual value of St. Paul's real property in 1883 was $79,058,430. But it is the per cent of increase, as indicated by the official figures, which illustrates and proves the city's wonderful growth since 1881. It will be remembered, by those who have read the preceding pages and the statistics given, that St. Paul's phenomenal growth has been since 1880; or since the railways, banks and commercial interests discovered the advantages of St. Paul's location above any other Northwestern city, and began to concentrate here. Now, this general theory is proved conclusively by the assessment rolls of the city of St. Paul, which show that while the official valuation of real property in 1881 was $21,595,326, in 1874 it was $21,361,774. In other words, while the official valuation increased only $233,552 in the seven years from 1874 to 1881, it increased $10,038,047 in the two years from 1881 to 1883. That is, the increase in the past *two* years was *over forty-two times greater* than the increase in the *seven* years preceding the beginning of St. Paul's recent growth. This showing, be it remembered, is from official figures. It must also be remembered that this is not the record of a small town, that may show great percentage of growth by the expenditure of a very little money, or the erection of a few houses, but is what has been accomplished by a city that contained over 40,000 inhabitants when its phenomenal development began. No city of like size — not excepting Chicago in its days of greatest prosperity — has ever equaled St. Paul's record of growth within the past three years. Inasmuch as the present year, 1884, seems certain to surpass any other twelvemonth, and there is no reason to doubt indefinite growth, what is to be expected of St. Paul's development during the next five or ten years? It is certainly not too much to expect that before the present decade is ended, St. Paul will outstrip Cincinnati in metropolitan importance, and be disputing with St. Louis and New Orleans the honor of supremacy among the cities of the Mississippi valley.

THE WHOLESALE DRY GOODS HOUSE OF LINDEKES, WARNER & SCHUEMEIER, CORNER FOURTH AND SIBLEY STREETS.

Public Libraries.

There are three public libraries in St. Paul that would do credit to much older and larger towns. The free library of the city contains between nine thousand and ten thousand volumes, and is supported by public tax. It is a new educational venture on the part of the city, and is therefore in its infancy; but it is increasing in number of volumes so rapidly that it must soon take rank among the large institutions of its class. It is furnished with every modern convenience for the ease and intellectual delight of those who make use of its spacious reading rooms.

The State library consists of ten thousand volumes, and is open to visitors daily from nine o'clock A. M. to six P. M. The library is located in the State capitol. Its catalogue is chiefly of law books and State documents.

The State historical library is located in the capitol building, and is open daily to visitors. It contains nearly twenty-two thousand volumes and pamphlets, together with a museum and cabinet of historical relics, pictures, portraits, curiosities, etc.

Lumber Trade.

The wholesale lumber trade of St. Paul is increasing with almost wonderful rapidity. The total sales in 1881 aggregated $1,348,000, while in 1883 the amount reached $3,600,000, or an increase of over 160 per cent within two years. This remarkable increase is largely due to recently acquired railway facilities — which will be quadrupled within two years — for reaching the Wisconsin pineries. Northern Iowa, Nebraska and Kansas are gradually forsaking the Chicago lumber market for that of St. Paul. Chicago, for many years, has been the greatest lumber mart in the world, handling upwards of 2,000,000,000 feet annually. During the past year, however, the Chicago sales have fallen off materially, while the St. Paul trade has increased as above indicated. In the chapter devoted to the country tributary to St. Paul, the reader will find detailed the facts relative to this city's position with reference to the lumber trade of Wisconsin. It will be noted that the St. Paul railway system is penetrating the pineries in such manner that every district in Northern Wisconsin will speedily acknowledge this city as its nearest and best market. It all means that St. Paul is soon to supersede Chicago as the market for Wisconsin lumber; and that, in turn, means that this city is to become the chief distributing point for the vast products of the sister State. At this time St. Paul lumbermen are beginning to ship as far southwest as Kansas City. Leading firms here state that far more capital than they now control could be used to great advantage in the St. Paul lumber trade. There are twenty-three firms in the lumber business in this city, and opportunities for as many more as will be required to handle the bulk of the Wisconsin cut within two or three years from the present time. The fact that nearly four thousand houses were built in St. Paul last year indicates what the local trade is.

With reference to the future magnitude of St. Paul's lumber trade, it must be considered that there are yet (by recent estimates) thirty-five or forty billion feet of standing pine in Northern Wisconsin, and that even at the present rate of cutting, the supply cannot be exhausted in very many years, as the constant growth is equal to a fair proportion of the amount logged. The present lumber product of Wisconsin is over 2,000,000,000 feet annually, and with the railway facilities that will be perfected this year, the entire region of product will be accessible from St. Paul. In addition to the Wisconsin lumber supply is that of Minnesota, which is just beginning to be developed, and which, in time, with the aid of railways now projected, will be tributary to this city.

Newspapers of the City.

The general character, appearance and professional rank of the newspapers of a city constitute a sure guide in estimating its people, their intelligence and their prosperity. Chicago was no less phenomenal in its newspaper development than in its commercial growth. The Eastern press was taught more lessons in enterprise by the Chicago journals than were the Eastern merchants by the energetic young business men of the Western metropolis. Just now we find the general development of Chicago ten or fifteen years ago duplicated in St. Paul. It is evidenced in its newspapers as in other lines. Go where you will in the United

THE PIONEER PRESS BUILDING.

The above cut represents a portion of the Third St. front of the PIONEER PRESS Co's building. The entire structure is 113 ft. front on Third St., 170 ft. on Minnesota, and 145 on Second, with irregular height of 4 and 5 stories. The concern is one of the most complete printing houses in the country.

States to-day, and in journalistic circles St. Paul will be ranked among the first newspaper towns of the country. This result is not to be attributed wholly to either the progress of the town or the character of the newspapers, for each has assisted in the upbuilding of the other; each are examples of Northwestern energy, and the talent — business or literary — that is generated by action is the result of such energy. St. Paul is acknowledged to have no equal in the Northwest in the line of newspaper enterprise, and has no superior in the country. Indeed, Chicago is the only city on the continent outside of St. Paul, that has what may be termed a perfect daily newspaper — the term including news and editorial facilities, make-up, mechanical resources, etc. There are four daily newspapers published in St. Paul, three English and one German; and all are prosperous and progressive. *The Pioneer Press* is issued every day in the year. It is seven columns quarto, with two, four, or eight-page supplements nearly every other day. It is circulated — not merely carried — over ten thousand miles of railroad daily. It is independent Republican in politics. *The Globe* is an eight-column quarto, with a flexible make-up which enables enlargement whenever necessary, and is the leading Democratic newspaper in the Northwest. The evening paper is the *St. Paul Dispatch*, a seven-column folio, which issues several editions during the afternoon. Recent enlargement indicates prosperity. It is republican in politics, and is the leading evening paper in the Northwest. The German daily is *Die Volkszeitung*, issued every week-day evening, and is the leading representative among the German press of the Northwest.

In addition to the daily press, there are fifteen weeklies and class publications, including German, French, Norwegian and Swedish newspapers.

So far as news gathering and printing facilities are concerned, the St. Paul dailies are unsurpassed. They have their own special wires to Chicago and Washington, and use the latest improved Webb perfecting presses in printing editions which circulate throughout the entire Northwest.

The Outlook for 1884.

The figures presented and statements made in foregoing pages refer in greater part to the business of 1883 and immediately preceding years; foreshadowing or indicating, merely, results likely to obtain in 1884 and the immediate future. The season is now far enough advanced, the latter part of March, to warrant definite conclusions with reference to the general growth and development of the city during the current year. At this time there is greater activity in building than has ever before been noted in St. Paul during a corresponding season. Go where one may, either in the business section or residence localities, and hardly a block of ground will be found — unless already compactly built — that does not present an active building scene. Scores of grand business structures are progressing in all stages of construction, from foundation walls to interior finishing work. In the residence districts over one thousand dwellings, including all classes, are now in process of erection; while every day adds many to the number. Architects who estimated three months ago that 1884 would surpass 1883 in general upbuilding, now unhesitatingly say that the record of last year will be surpassed at least thirty per cent. This means that St. Paul will witness this year the erection of at least five thousand new buildings; and if this proves to be a nearly correct estimate, it is quite certain that New York and Chicago alone of all the cities of America will surpass St. Paul's building growth for the present year. It will even prove interesting and instructive for old residents of St. Paul to make frequent drives about town — especially in the outlying districts — and note the marvelous development now going on. Everywhere outside of the long-built-up portion of the city, houses, stores, shops and factories are springing up as if by magic.

INFLUX OF POPULATION.

Two months ago, owing to the large number of houses built last year, it was generally believed that the influx of people this spring could not possibly be so great as to make dwellings actually scarce; yet at this writing it is estimated that if there were now one thousand houses placed for rent, all would be taken within a fortnight. This does not mean that it is impossible to secure living accommodations at reasonable rates, for it has become the rule to rent parts of houses for temporary purposes until houses approaching completion can be made ready for occupancy. That is, so many new structures are constantly building that the inconvenience of living in close quarters is merely temporary. But the fact that dwellings at this time are actually scarce, despite the number built last year, is evidence of the multitude of newcomers now seeking residence in this prosperous city. Not only is present immigration to St. Paul and the Northwest very large, but all indications go to show that a great tidal wave of humanity is to surge in this direction all through the year.

INCOMING CAPITAL.

The season thus far assures for the year a large increase of capital in every line of business and investment. Men of money from all parts of the Union are begin-

THE COURT BLOCK, FOURTH STREET.

The above block, erected by Comodore W. F. Davidson, is now being completed. It is six stories high, 75 feet front by 65 deep with a pressed brick front, cost about $75,000 and is designed for an office building with stores below.

ning to arrive for the purpose of investigating the opportunities presented for profitable use of capital ; and, as a rule, but little time is required to discover satisfactory chances. In regard to amount of new capital invested, it is altogether likely that 1884 will surpass any other year in St. Paul's history.

INVESTMENTS IN REALTY.

Judging from present indications — based largely upon letters of inquiry received from the East and South by real estate agents — a great many capitalists have concluded to make permanent investments in St. Paul. The present growth of the city, with its certain future, is noted, and then it is easy to comprehend that in view of these conditions prices of all kinds of property are very low. Capitalists are beginning to appreciate the absolute certainty of St. Paul's becoming one of the greatest trade centers of the continent, and are therefore preparing to invest in realty while values are yet much below those ruling in any other town of like population, to say nothing of future prospects.

The Wealthy Men of the City

It is a trueism that "what has been done, may be done again." Apply the hypothesis to the financial attainments of a majority of the leading business men of St. Paul, and there is an irresistable attraction in the corollary to any energetic young man ; for the wealth of the larger number of the city's millionaries has been wrought out of opportunities presented here. St. Paul has ever been a field where application of energy and brains has resulted in abundant success and prosperity. With very few exceptions the citizens of great wealth have made all their money in St. Paul. From inconsequential beginnings have resulted — and in comparatively few years — great and powerful railway corporations, mighty banking institutions, almost unsurpassed commercial houses, large manufactures, retail establishments that vie with the best of much larger cities, and newspaper product that is famous the country over. In every line of business great fortunes have been carved out of mere development of surroundings. What has been done may not only be done again, but inasmuch as St. Paul's growth is now more rapid than ever before, there is at this time better opportunities than have been presented in the past.

Secret Societies.

Secret societies are well represented in St. Paul. Here is the Grand Lodge of the Masons of Minnesota, with fifteen subordinate lodges, etc., and the Masonic Relief Association of the State. The respective Masonic societies are: Grand Lodge of the State; Grand Chapter; Royal Arch Chapter; Grand Commandery; Damascus Commandery; Grand Council of Royal and Select Masters ; Carmel Lodge of Perfection: A. and A. S. Rite: De Molai Council, Knights Kadosh, A. and A. S. Rite; Minnesota Consistory : St. Paul Chapter, Knights Rose Croix ; St. Paul Council : St. Paul Lodge ; Ancient Landmark Lodge ; Pioneer Lodge ; and Colored F. and A. M.

Of Odd Fellows there are six lodges and the Grand Lodge of the State : the Grand Encampment of Minnesota ; Minnesota Encampment No. 1; St. Paul Encampment No. 15 ; St. Paul Temple No. 2, Patriarchal Circle ; and Odd Fellows' Mutual Benefit Society.

Knights of Pythias are represented by a Grand Lodge of the State, Champion Lodge, and Section 159 Endowment Rank.

Other societies and orders are : Ancient Order of Hibernians, three divisions ; Ancient Order United Workmen, Grand Lodge and eight subordinate lodges ; Sons of Hermann, Grand Lodge and three subordinate lodges : Independent Order B'nai B'rith : two lodges of Knights of Honor two lodges Knights of Labor ; Grand Grove of United Ancient Order of Druids, and six subordinate groves.

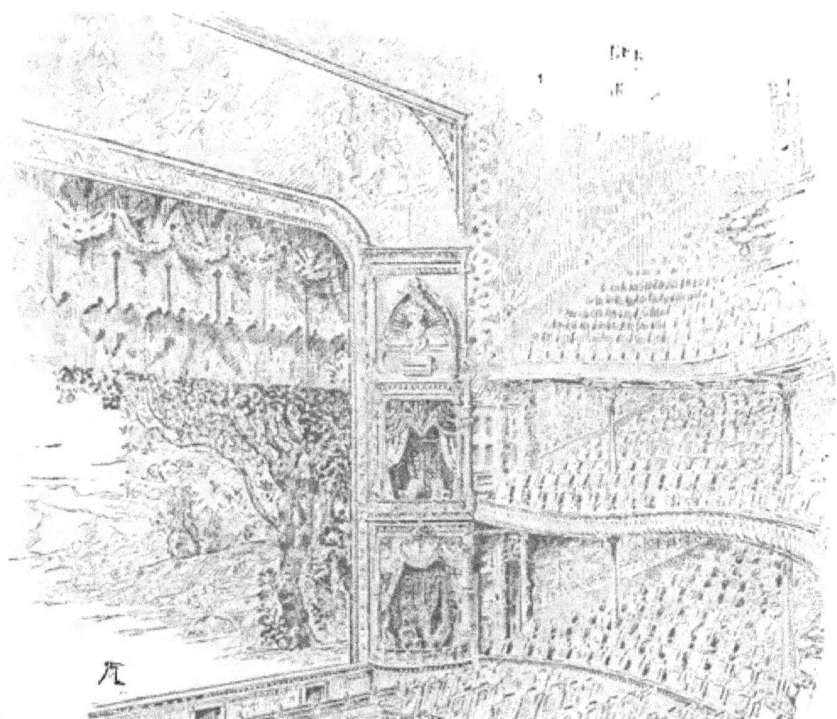

The above sketch is of a section of the auditorium, dress circle and balcony, with the stage opening, in the new Grand Opera House, completed and opened last year by Commodore Wm. F. Davidson; L. N. Scott, Manager. Its entrance is through a wide and convenient hall, running level from the sidewalk to the foyer. Its seating capacity is 2,200, and the ventilation, light (electricity being used), convenience of egress, safety and general appointments are equal to that of any theater in Chicago, and superior to any northwest of that city. It is pronounced by professionals equal to many of the finest opera houses of Eastern cities, and is specially commended for its excellent acoustic properties. The Fourth street front, known as "Court Block," is six stories high, faced with pressed brick, and being furnished for an office building. The Wabasha street front (old Opera House) will be remodeled, and when completed will present an elegant front six stories high. The entire improvement connected with the Grand Opera House occupies 85 feet front on Wabasha street by 225 feet deep, and 105 feet front on Fourth by 65 feet deep, both fronts being six stories high. The entire plant, including ground, old Opera House, new Grand Opera House, the Economy Sham Heat Co., and Court Block, is valued at half a million dollars, and brings an annual income of from fifty to sixty thousand dollars.

Amusements.

The new Grand Opera House, built in 1883 by Commodore W. F. Davidson, is one of the most beautiful and commodious theaters in the country. It is the largest building of its class in the Northwest, and rivals in interior art work and elegance of furnishing the leading theaters of Chicago. Visitors are invariably surprised to find here a place of amusement so far above the average of those of American cities, while the operatic and theatrical professions are invariably loud in their praise of the accoustic, stage and general properties of the St. Paul Grand. The leading stage talent of the country consider this city one of the best and most appreciative points in the entire circle of operatic or dramatic starring tours.

WINDSOR HOTEL, CORNER ST. PETER AND FIFTH STREETS.

Opportunities for Investing Capital

If St. Paul is now the most rapidly growing city on the continent and bids fair to become one of the chief commercial, railway and financial centers of America, it follows as a self-evident proposition that it presents the best and most varied field for the investment of capital. The almost innumerable lines or opportunities that may be followed or utilized have been fairly indicated in preceding pages; but there are salient points which may be reiterated to the advantage of those who seek monetary investment:

Two of St. Paul's greatest needs at this time are store or office accommodations for business, and dwellings for incoming population. Capitalists may count with certainty that on an outlay of $15,000 to $20,000 for business sites and $50,000 to $100,000 in superstructure erected thereon they will receive in rentals from $10,000 to $25,000. There is not only immediate, but constantly increasing need of business blocks. Sites may now be secured at from $150 to $450 per front foot that will undoubtedly be worth twice or thrice these prices within from two to five years.

In the present month, March, 1884, there is so great a demand for dwellings that if there were now one thousand new houses for rent they would all be taken within two weeks. Lots costing from $600 to $1,500, with dwellings averaging from $1,000 to $2,500 cost, can be rented quickly for $18 to $35 per month. The residence sites are just as certain to increase in value as the city is to continue to grow.

Every line of wholesale trade or manufactures offers better inducements here than at any other place, as the shrewd business man may quickly and easily determine for himself by examination of the general field.

In real estate investments there is an opportunity probably never before equaled for reasonably certain profits. Prices for all kinds of realty are very low as compared with other cities of not near St. Paul's present commercial rank and population, to say nothing of future prospects. Five hundred dollars per front foot is as yet about the limit of choice business frontage, while at various points in the business section prices range from $125 to $250 per front foot. Residence lots and suburban property may be considered safe and paying investments.

The time to make money in St. Paul is *now*, when the average man has hardly awakened to a realizing sense of what the future greatness of St. Paul and the Northwest is to be.

President John B. Sanborn's Address.

ADDRESS OF JOHN B. SANBORN ESQ., PRESIDENT OF THE SAINT PAUL CHAMBER OF COMMERCE, DELIVERED BEFORE THE BOARD OF DIRECTORS AT THE REGULAR MEETING, MARCH 24, 1884.

Gentlemen of the Board of Directors:—The year 1883 has been one of unprecedented activity, and we hope of unprecedented usefulness, of this organization.

The modification of our by-laws in such manner as would authorize you to raise means to purchase a suitable building site and construct a Chamber of Commerce building ; reorganization under these amended by-laws ; securing perpetual memberships and providing means to purchase a building site; consideration and adoption of plans for the new building ; forming and giving expression to a proper public sentiment in regard to local and public improvements, and the best time and manner of their construction : careful examination of the general plans and policy of the federal government in making improvements to cheapen transportation of commodities between the various seaports and the interior of our continent, by extending and improving the navigable water ways of the country ; giving whatever of aid was possible to assist the proper officers to reduce the expenses of the city government to the lowest point consistent with due protection to person and property, with a view to diminish the rate of taxation; giving suitable tone and emphasis to the great event of the decade in the Northwest.— the completion and opening to traffic of the Northern Pacific railroad from this city to the navigable waters of the Pacific ocean and giving due publicity to such expression in connection with a history of our past growth and present condition ; raising and forwarding money and other substantial aid to the many sufferers by extraordinary storms—constitute some of the matters which, in addition to the minor details of business attended to at all your regular sessions, have received your attention the past year.

It will demonstrate your public spirit, as well as that of our people generally, to refer to the fact that, in our membership of the board of directors of forty-two, of which a majority of all is necessary to transact business, and under by-laws requiring a meeting every Monday morning at nine o'clock, a quorum has responded at the roll call of that hour on every Monday morning of the year. Such men deserve success, and fortunate is the city that includes them among her citizens.

The financial operations of the Chamber were much larger in 1883 than for any previous year, but were attended with no friction or trouble. The receipts from all sources, not including money raised for charitable purposes, were as follows :

RECEIPTS.

Fines...$	62.00
Rents...	1,538.24
Annual memberships...	1,035.00
Perpetual memberships..	800.00
First call of 50 per cent of bonds of perpetual members............................	19,000.00
Old paper sold...	4.13
Aggregate receipts..$	31,459.37

DISBURSEMENTS.

The disbursements for the same period have been as follows, viz. :

Indebtedness paid...$	2,409.66
Rent...	1,000.00
Expenses other than salary..	1,553.79
Salary of secretary...	958.33
For real estate (building site)...	25,000.00
Building account...	127.50
Leaving cash on hand (in bank)...	410.09
Total..$	31,459.37

CURRENT YEAR EXPENSES.

The estimated amount required to meet all the demands upon the Chamber the current year are as follows :

Expenses of Chamber, including the salary of the secretary.........................$	3,000.00
Rent for present premises..	1,200.00
For construction of new building...	100,000.00
Total..$104,200.00	

CURRENT YEAR RESOURCES.

The estimated resources for 1884 are as follows :

Annual memberships..$	2,000.00
Perpetual membership assessments...	1,000.00
Rents..	1,500.00
Bonds agreed to be taken by present perpetual members............................	34,000.00
First mortgage on building and site..	50,000.00
Amount of deficit to be raised from additional perpetual members, or from additional bonds taken by the present perpetual members...................................	15,700.00
Total..$104,200.00	

It is estimated by our building committee that the rents of the new building will pay interest on the entire cost of the property, all repairs thereon, and expenses of the same—the ordinary expenses of the Chamber—and leave at least $3,000 a year, to be used as a sinking fund, to extinguish the debt incurred to perpetual members and others for money to purchase the site and build the building.

The necessities of the Chamber for the year 1884 will be large, as shown above, and will no doubt be met with that public spirit and liberality which is so characteristic of our people, and which has done so much to make this city the metropolis of the Northwest.

STATISTICS OF GROWTH.

The report of your secretary and committee on statistics and publication, which is herewith transmitted, is complete in the details of our growth in population, in wealth, in buildings and other improvements, and replete with information concerning the past growth and future prospects of the city, and is commended for the careful examination of all having any interest in our past history, present condition, or future development. This report shows conclusively that the year 1883 was, to Saint Paul, one of wonderful improvement and prosperity. There was a great

JEFFERSON SCHOOL.—AN AVERAGE PUBLIC SCHOOL BUILDING.

increase in all branches of business. The wholesale trade reached $72,048,771, while this branch in 1882 reached but $66,628,494. The price of goods was much less in the latter than the former year, so that the increase greatly exceeds what is shown simply by the value of goods sold. The increase in the value of coal and iron sold is $1,469,666, and in several other commodities is little less striking. The number of wholesale houses increased from two hundred and seventy-six in 1882. to three hundred and twenty-five in 1883, and the number of persons employed in this business increased from four thousand six hundred and eighty-five in 1882, to five thousand eight hundred and fifteen in 1883.

The increase shown in manufacturing industries, by these statistics, is no less striking than that of the wholesale trade. The number of manufacturing establishments increased from six hundred and ninety-four in 1882, to seven hundred and fifty-eight in 1883, and the number of persons employed in this industry increased from twelve thousand two hundred and sixty-seven in 1882, to thirteen thousand nine hundred and seventy-nine in 1883, and the value of the products of manufacture increased from $22,390,589 to $25,885,471 in the same time.

The amount of capital shown to have been invested in buildings during this year is $11,935,950, which was exceeded by only three cities of the United States, viz.: New York, Chicago and Cincinnati. This capital was so divided as to give us about two miles of additional fronts of business houses, and eight miles of additional fronts of residences. The death rate for the year was only 11.65 to each 1,000 of population, which is less than the general average of the State, and less than that of any other city containing so large a population in the world.

Capital has been augmented to meet the increasing demands of our growing commerce and manufactures until the banking capital and business of the city exceeds that of all other cities and towns in the State of Minnesota combined, reaching the sum of $5,550,000 of capital stock, with deposits exceeding $11,000,000, and annual sale of exchange reaching the enormous aggregate of over $100,000,000.

The officers of our city have generally shown zeal, ability and integrity in the discharge of their respective duties, and, although there is room for improvement, as there always must be while the infirmities of human nature remain, still we may congratulate ourselves that no city anywhere has a government better administered than Saint Paul. The public debt has not yet reached more than five per cent of the fair valuation of the property of the city subject to assessment and taxation, although we have passed the point where extraordinary expenditures are required in aid of railroads coming to the city ; or to establish and put in operation a sewerage system ; or to purchase and extend the operation of a proper system to provide water for all portions of the city ; or to purchase school building sites and buildings thereon ; or to erect many costly iron bridges over ravines, rivers and streams. All these extraordinary expenses have been incurred and paid.

MATTERS OF PUBLIC POLICY.

The matters which most demand, and which are now receiving the attention of the proper officers of the city, are the extension of the sewerage and water systems to the fourth, fifth, and sixth wards, and replacing the old plank sidewalks with stone on all our business streets. Both public and private interests demand that a city of one hundred thousand people, transacting a business of more than $100,000,000 annually, should not tolerate or be disgraced with such sidewalks on its business streets longer.

The commercial and business character of our people causes them to take a deep interest in all that pertains to the public welfare, as thereby they become connected with the general business of the county, and knowing that one part of the same body cannot be sound while another remains unsound. To those in whose memories there still linger a recollection of the uncertainties, dangers, and losses attending all business transactions before the war, resulting from an unsound and inflated currency issued by State banks chartered and doing business under as many different systems as there were different States, any suggestion of a radical

Bridge over the Mississippi

change or thought of the abandonment of the present financial policy and banking system of the federal government is nothing less than a menace and threat of destruction to the business interests and prosperity of the country. The financial and banking system of the nation, engendered by the dire financial necessities of war, has proved an unspeakable blessing to all the business men and interests of this country, and should be preserved for all time and looked upon by all classes as one of the chief blessings transmitted to us from that period of gloom and destruction. That there is still room for improvement there can be no doubt, in some details, but when we consider the imperfections of human judgment we must conclude that change is more likely to be for the worse instead of the better.

A MEMORABLE YEAR.

The year just past will always remain one of the most memorable in the annals of the city. It has witnessed the completion of the new capitol building and new opera house, and the commencement of the new $1,000,000 hotel, new court house, and new Chamber of Commerce building. To all this the mind instinctively connects the completion of the Northern Pacific railroad, which, together, make it a year never to be forgotten. From it the city dates a new era. The vast new and fertile regions thereby opened to settlement and business, all tributary to the navigable waters of the Mississippi and to the commerce of our city, removes all limit to our growth and development. The facilities for doing business here are not surpassed any where. Eight trains leave daily for Chicago and the East : four for Manitoba and the Northwest, independent of the Northern Pacific : two for Portland, Ore., and all intermediate points: four for the navigable waters of Lake Superior, two for St. Louis, and not less than six for the West, Southwest and South. each carrying through cars to the commercial and political capitals of all adjacent States and Territories, while the whole number of passenger trains that run in and out of the city daily is one hundred and sixty-four. The Wisconsin Central, Minnesota & Northwestern, St. Paul Eastern, Grand Trunk, Winona, Alma and Northern, Chicago, Burlington & Quincy, and Chicago & Rock Island, are all taking steps to extend their lines to this metropolis at an early day.

The Northern Pacific Railroad Company, the St. Paul, Minneapolis & Manitoba Railroad Company, the Chicago, St. Paul, Minneapolis & Omaha Railroad Company, each operating long lines of completed road, have erected elegant buildings for their main offices in this city, and from the mall the operations of these lines of road are carried on.

THE FUTURE OF THE CITY.

It therefore seems proper that I should give expression to a sentiment that must be common to us all, that at no period has the future of this city been so bright with promise as now. It seems miraculous, even to those who have stood by and watched and participated in all the past events of its development, that, notwithstanding the great financial crash of 1857, that in a single month swept away all the wealth and much of the growth of the first eight years of its existence — and the exhausting and destructive influences of the great rebellion and Indian wars that came upon our people before they had commenced to rally from the disasters of 1857, and which for five long years continued to absorb all the energies of our people, still in the short space of thirty-five years there has grown up here the city of to-day. Thirty-five years ago no city, no railroad, no street, no highway, no church, no school-house, no home — nothing but earth, air and water, common to all and enjoyed only by savage and uncultivated life — to-day, the one hundred thousand people, the $100,000,000 of business, church edifices of magnificent structure and proportions; the elegant school-houses, the mansion and residence, the comforts and refinements of the highest type of civilized life.

With the growth of the last thirty-five years before us, under circumstances so adverse, what may we not expect in the next period of equal duration? All the country about us, east, west, north and south has, by our railroad system, been

SECTION OF GILFILLAN BLOCK, IN WHOLESALE DISTRICT, ON FOURTH STREET
BETWEEN JACKSON AND SIBLEY STREETS.

connected with and made tributary to us.   This country which to-day is occupied
by the pioneer settlers who first entered it, must soon all be filled up and culti-
vated by an intelligent and industrious population.   The wealth and products of
remote States and Territories and the commerce of distant continents will long ere
this period shall have passed be poured into our lap.

We see more growth and increase in the city in a single year now than in a
whole decade of its early history; we see a country now tributary to its commerce
and business capable of supporting twenty times its present population, and we
see our business men and interests keeping pace with and growing up with all this
surrounding country.   All things now conspire to maintain and enlarge the present
commercial and manufacturing supremacy of the city and add to its business and
wealth till it shall have few superiors or equals on this continent.

St. Paul Chamber of Commerce.

OFFICERS OF THE ST. PAUL CHAMBER OF COMMERCE FOR 1883-4:

President . . . . Gen. John B. Sanborn.
Vice-President . . . . Frederick Driscoll. .
Secretary . . . . C. A. McNeale.
Treasurer . . . . Peter Berkey.

BOARD OF DIRECTORS:

J. T. Averill,	S. S. Glidden,	W. P. Murray,
T. J. Barney,	C. Gotzian,	D. R. Noyes,
P. Berkey,	H. Greve,	C. D. O'Brien,
J. W. Bishop,	J. P. Gribben,	A. Oppenheim.
R. Blakeley,	E. J. Hodgson,	J. C. Quinby,
H. A. Castle,	D. W. Ingersoll,	Edmund Rice,
T. Cochran, Jr.,	W. Lee.	L. W. Rundlett.
J. H. Davidson,	W. Lindeke,	John B. Sanborn.
W. F. Davidson,	J. D. Ludden,	W. A. Somers,
D. Day,	J. J. McCardy,	L. K. Stone,
E. F. Drake,	J. W. McClung,	C. D. Strong,
F. Driscoll,	T. S. McManus,	C. B. Thurston,
F. A. Fogg,	John Matheis,	W. A. Van Slyke,
J. M. Gilman,	D. H. Moon,	F. Willius.

STANDING COMMITTEES, 1883-4.

Executive Committee—F. Driscoll, C. D. O'Brien, Edmund Rice, Peter Berkey, Herman Greve, W. F. Davidson, Daniel R. Noyes, William Lindeke, John T. Averill, Thomas Cochran, Jr., J. W. Bishop, F. Willius, F. A. Fogg, H. A. Castle, J. W. McClung.

Statistics and Correspondence—David Day, Thomas Cochran, Jr., H. A. Castle.

Finance—Peter Berkey, F. Willius, A. Oppenheim.

Mercantile Committee—D. R. Noyes, D. W. Ingersoll, J. D. Ludden, D. H. Moon, C. B. Thurston.

Manufactures—T. J. Barney, J. P. Gribben, J. C. Quinby.

Transportation—J. W. Bishop, J. H. Davidson, S. S. Glidden.

Mississippi River—W. F. Davidson, R. Blakeley, Edmund Rice, Ansel Oppenheim, W. A. Van Slyke, W. P. Murray, C. Gotzian, J. M. Gilman, C. D. Strong, T. J. Barney.

Streets, Roads and Parks—J. W. McClung, W. A. Van Slyke, L. W. Rundlett, W. A. Somers, E. J. Hodgson.

Health and Sanitation—E. J. Hodgson, F. Willius, T. S. McManus.

Buildings and Fire Department—E. F. Drake, C. Gotzian, William Lee.

Taxes, County and City Officials—William Lee, Frederick Driscoll, Peter Berkey.

General Improvement—C. D. Strong, John Matheis, T. S. McManus.

Legislative Committee—W. P. Murray, John M. Gilman, J. H. Davidson.

Auditing Committee—J. J. McCardy, Ansel Oppenheim.

Nominations—D. W. Ingersoll, W. A. Van Slyke, Thomas Cochran, Jr., D. H. Moon, William Lindeke.

Market House—D. R. Noyes, P. Berkey, H. A. Castle.

PERPETUAL MEMBERS OF THE ST. PAUL CHAMBER OF COMMERCE.

J. Q. Adams,
M. Auerbach,
J. T. Averill,
A. K. Barnum,
B. Beaupre,
J. A. Berkey,
Peter Berkey,
J. W. Bishop,
R. Blakeley,
E. A. Brown,
H. A. Castle,
Greenleaf Clark,
F. B. Clarke,
Thos. Cochran, Jr.,
H. S. Crippen,
J. H. Davidson,
W. F. Davidson,
W. Dawson,
A. De Graff,
C. E. Dickerman,
W. T. Donaldson,
R. R. Dorr,
F. Driscoll,
E. S. Edgerton,
H. S. Fairchild,
Geo. R. Finch,
C. E. Flandrau,

F. A. Fogg,
R. B. Galusha,
Cass Gilbert,
R. Jordan,
C. Gotzian,
H. Greve,
J. P. Gribben,
H. P. Hall,
D. W. Hand,
Springer Harbaugh,
P. R. L. Hardenberg,
G. S. Heron,
Chester G. Higbee,
Matt Holl,
D. W. Ingersoll,
H. C. James,
R. W. Johnson,
E. H. Judson,
A. Kalman,
P. H. Kelly,
Frank Keogh,
A. R. Kiefer,
N. W. Kittson,
James King,
Uri L. Lamprey,
C. H. Lineau,
W. Lindeke,

J. D. Ludden,
J. J. McCardy,
T. S. McManus,
S. R. McMasters,
E. Mannheimer,
John Matheis,
J. L. Merriam,
W. R. Merriam,
D. D. Merrill,
D. H. Moon,
C. A. Moore,
W. S. Morton,
Stanford Newel,
E. S. Norton,
D. R. Noyes,
H. O'Gorman,
John B. Olivier,
A. Oppenheim,
E. F. Osborne,
W. L. Perkins,
G. H. Ranney,
P. Reilly,
W. Rhodes,
Edmund Rice,
Edmund Rice, Jr.,
W. G. Robertson,

E. G. Rogers,
J. N. Rogers,
J. B. Sanborn,
W. H. Sanborn,
E. N. Saunders,
Albert Scheffer,
C. H. Schlick,
T. L. Schurmeier,
C. Seabury,
Ed. Simonton,
Jas. Smith, Jr.,
Kingsland Smith,
R. A. Smith,
N. E. Solomon,
F. R. Sterrett,
A. B. Stickney,
G. C. Stone,
H. E. Thompson,
W. A. Van Slyke,
Lucien Warner,
J. J. Watson,
J. A. Wheelock,
A. H. Wilder,
F. Willius,
Gustav Willius,
W. C. Wilson.

LIST OF ANNUAL MEMBERS — 1883-4.

T. A. Abbott & Co,
D. Aberle & Co.,
Albenburg & Couhaim,
J. H. Amos,
Arthur, Warren & Abbott,
Bacon & Stone,
T. J. Barney,
George Benz & Co.,
S. Bergman,
E. F. Berrisford,
C. H. Bigelow,
H. R. Bigelow,
E. H. Biggs,
Blodgett & Osgood,
Bohrer & Hullsick,
Bristol, Smith & Freeman,
J. H. Burwell,
Campbell & Burbank,
Carpenter & Teltz,
Clark & Frost,
Gordon E. Cole,
W. Constans,
E. W. Corning,
Craig, Larkin & Smith,
Ammi Cutter,
Merell, Sahlgaard & Thwing,
Monfort & Co.,
C. F. Mould,
R. C. Munger,
W. P. Murray,
Nicols & Dean,
C. D. O'Brien,
Harvey Officer,
George Palmes,
J. F. Pannell & Co.,
A. M. Peabody,
H. L. Pilkington & Co.,
Samuel Potter,
B. Presley & Co.,
A. K. Pruden,
A. Pugh,
Quinby & Hallowell,

C. K. Davis,
David Day,
De Coster & Clark,
F. R. Delano,
E. F. Drake,
J. H. Drake,
R. G. Dun & Co.,
Dyer & Howard,
P. F. Egan & Co,
A. S. Elfelt,
H. N. Elmer,
Farwell, Ozmun & Jackson,
Nathan Ford,
Forepaugh & Tarbox,
J. G. Freeman & Co.,
C. D. Gilfillan,
J. M. Gilman,
S. S. Glidden,
Graves & Vinton,
C. R. Groff,
H. S. Haas,
H. Habighorst,
Theodore Hamm,
G. H. Hazzard,
Gustave Heinemann,
Ransom & Horton,
Robinson & Carey,
J. W. Routh,
H. P. Rugg & Co.
L. W. Rundlett,
Merrell Ryder,
Sattler Bros.,
Schultz, Becht & Hospes,
F. J. Schultz,
J. M. Schulze & Macdonald,
G. E. Skinner,
Karl Simmon,
Smith Bros. & Erskine,
W. A. Somers,
J. Walter Stevens,
A. J. Stone,
C. D. Strong,

J. J. Hill,
E. J. Hodgson,
H. Houlton,
Hoxsie & Jaggar,
Hubbard & Fay,
Kellogg, Johnson & Co.,
D. L. Kingsbury,
R. A. Kirk,
W. H. Konantz & Bros.,
A. L. Larpenteur,
William Lee & Co.,
Lichtenauer & Heinemann,
E. Lytle,
J. W. McClung,
McIlrath & Gilbert,
F. F. McIver,
Joseph McKey & Co.,
C. M. McLain,
J. T. McMillan,
C. A. McNeale,
Walter Mann,
W. R. Marshall,
Mathes, Good & Schurmeier,
Mayo & Clark,
T. N. Metcalf,
E. T. Sumwalt,
H. Swift,
H. S. Treherne,
C. B. Thurston,
H. P. Upham,
J. C. Wall,
Walsh & Goforth,
Eugene Ward,
W. P. Warner,
C. L. Willes,
George Wirth,
J. H. Woolsey,
Yanz & Howes,
Anthony Yoerg,
Young, Streissguth & Drake.

Index.

	Page.
Summary of Salient Features	3
Introductory	7
Site of St. Paul	8
St. Paul's Wholesale Trade	9
The Retail Trade	18
St. Paul's Manufactures	20
Hints to Manufacturers	24
Financial Center of the Northwest	36
Social Advantages	41
St. Paul's Railway System	42
Territory Tributary to St. Paul	50
Educational Facilities	54
St. Paul Churches	58
Remarkable Increase in Population	61
River Traffic	62
Building Review	63
Real Estate	65
Health of St. Paul	66
The General Climate of Minnesota	67
Suburban Attractions	69
Cost of Living in St. Paul	74
Postoffice Statistics	75
A Word to Workingmen	76
Building and Loan Associations	76
Increase in Value of Realty	78
Public Libraries	79
Lumber Trade	80
The Newspapers of the City	80
The Outlook for 1884	81
The Wealthy Men of the City	84
Secret Societies	84
Amusements	85
Opportunities for Investing Capital	86
President Sanborn's Address	87
Officers of Chamber of Commerce	94

www.ingramcontent.com/pod-product-compliance
Lightning Source LLC
Chambersburg PA
CBHW021409090426
42742CB00009B/1069